TERRORISM
How the West Can Win

TERRORISM
How the West Can Win

EDITED BY
Benjamin Netanyahu

FARRAR · STRAUS · GIROUX

NEW YORK

Library of Congress Cataloging-in-Publication Data
Terrorism: how the West can win.
1. Terrorism—Addresses, essays, lectures.
2. Terrorism—Prevention—Addresses, essays, lectures.
I. Netanyahu, Binyamin.
HV6431.T466   1986   363.3'2   85–31225

The author is grateful to the contributors for their
generous cooperation and support in the publication
of this book.
The royalties from the sale of this book are forwarded to
the Jonathan Institute, a nonprofit foundation,
so that it may continue its work in
the struggle against terrorism.

To my parents,
Cela and Benzion Netanyahu,
who taught us the meaning of courage

Acknowledgments

THIS is a twofold expression of thanks: First, to those who made possible the conference of the Jonathan Institute on whose proceedings this volume is based; second, to those who helped in the preparation of the book itself.

David Bar-Illan (who served as conference director) and Peter Lubin, with their wise counsel and prodigious talents, immeasurably helped in organizing the conference. I am grateful for their support as I am for their friendship.

Lord Chalfont, who chaired the conference with a graceful authority, deserves a particular expression of thanks. To David Shimron I owe a special debt for helping share the exhausting burden of running the conference itself. Moshe Decter, who took charge of press releases during the conference, also made many fine editing suggestions in several articles.

What must have appeared at times an endless task, the typing and retyping of this manuscript, was done in wonderful spirit by Rachel Leaf and Sharon Jacoby in Washington and by Aviva Mayer in New York; to each I owe warm thanks.

Not every editor is as lucky in his own editor as I was with mine. David Rieff of Farrar, Straus and Giroux not only sharpened and clarified many important points throughout the book but did so with wit and elegance. Working with him turned even the most mundane chores of editing into a pleasurable experience.

I owe, lastly, more than words to Fleur, whose discerning intelligence and intuition were matched only by her patience and support over many years.

Preface

THE PROBLEM of international terrorism was not as clearly understood in the 1970s as it is beginning to be today. Few people recognized the real sources of its alarming growth. Fewer still believed there were practical ways to fight terrorists and defeat them. The need for a better understanding of terrorism and for mobilizing the West against it were among the major considerations that in 1976 gave rise to the Jonathan Institute. The Fourth of July of that year marked the Entebbe rescue, which has since become the symbol of bold and successful action against international terrorism. My brother, Lieutenant Colonel Jonathan Netanyahu, led the rescue party and fell in this mission. The Jonathan Institute, a private research foundation concentrating, among other things, on terrorism, was established in his name, not merely because Jonathan fought and died in the war against terror. He, like other Israelis, devoted his efforts to protecting his country, but he also believed that the battle against terrorism was part of a much larger struggle, one between the forces of civilization and the forces of barbarism, and that, if left unchallenged, terrorism would continue to spread with disastrous consequences.

The main purpose of the Jonathan Institute is to bring this truth home to the governments and citizens of the free world. The institute sponsored two international conferences, five years apart, to examine the problem of terrorism and to suggest ways to combat it.

The first, held in Jerusalem on July 2–5, 1979, was attended by fifty statesmen, scholars, and journalists from a dozen countries. The Jerusalem conference exposed for the first time the full involvement of states in international terrorism, and the centrality of the Soviet Union and the PLO in fomenting and spreading it. For example, the former chief of Israeli military intelligence, General Shlomo Gazit, revealed that "Arab terrorists participated in fifty different military schools and courses in the Soviet bloc, some forty in the Soviet Union itself." The conference also predicted the rise of terrorist states, emphasizing the importance of the then newly established Islamic republic in Iran.

The events of the intervening years proved the accuracy of the conference's prognosis. International terrorism continued to escalate. The involvement of states and collaboration between groups became a commonplace, and was often admitted openly (for example, following Soviet denunciations of the conference's statements about Soviet training of the PLO, a PLO spokesman officially confirmed this on American television [PBS] on September 27, 1979). The pivotal role of the PLO in sponsoring and training terrorist groups from all over the world was fully unmasked by the wealth of documents and other evidence uncovered during Israel's action in Lebanon in 1982. And Iran's support for Islamic terrorists outside its border became apparent to the entire world from 1980 on.

Many observers believed that the Jerusalem conference was a turning point in the understanding of international terrorism. But though the conference helped focus the attention of influential circles in the West on the real nature of the terrorist threat, this was not enough. True, Western governments began to adopt a more vigorous stand toward terrorist attacks on their own soil and against their own nationals. But what was still lacking was a coherent and united *international* response. In its absence, terrorist assaults against the democracies increased in frequency, ferocity, and geographic scope.

To advocate such a unified policy and to suggest what it might consist of was the principal objective of the Jonathan Institute's second international gathering, held in Washington on June 24–27, 1984. This book is based on its proceedings. The views of the contributors, all conference participants, are not always identical. At times they might even conflict with one another on specific points. But they form an overriding consensus on the urgent need for the West to undertake a broad-based, vigorous campaign against the terrorists and their sponsors. While this campaign necessarily involves many different approaches, it is above all a *political* struggle, responding as it does to an assault which is essentially political in nature.

The West, the principal target of international terrorism, must organize itself for this battle. It must, and it can, adopt a variety of means—political, economic, and military—with which to fight back. But underlying them all must be the *moral* understanding that terrorism, under whatever guise or pretext, is an inexcusable evil, that it obliterates the political and moral distinctions which are the foundations of humane and free life under the rule of law; that the West, in short, must resist terrorism and ultimately defeat it. Hence the title of this book and its purpose.

Contents

IV / THE INTERNATIONAL NETWORK   85

V / TERRORISM AND THE MEDIA   109

VI / THE LEGAL FOUNDATIONS FOR THE WAR AGAINST TERRORISM   131

VII / THE DOMESTIC BATTLE   163

TERRORISM
How the West Can Win

Introduction

TO WIN THE WAR AGAINST TERRORISM, free societies must first know what they are fighting. This is why this book begins with what has been regarded as the most elusive but indispensable starting point—a definition of terrorism. It rejects absolutely the notion that "one man's terrorist is another man's freedom fighter" and presents clear ways of distinguishing terrorists, offering in effect a litmus test for terrorism and its practitioners.

It then examines the challenge that terrorism poses to the democracies of the West, which are its main targets—not only because they absorb the brunt of terrorist attacks, but because their political philosophy is anathema to the terrorists. The book then proceeds to examine more closely how the two main antagonists of democracy in the postwar world, communist totalitarianism and Islamic radicalism, have between them inspired virtually all of contemporary terrorism.

The practical outgrowth of these ideological and religious forces, the book shows, are states and groups which, taken together, form a worldwide network of terror. Some important examples of this network are given, though by no means exhaustively; that would require another book.

The main purpose of *this* book is to show how terrorism can be defeated. To achieve this purpose, the book focuses first on what the response of Western public opinion has been, and then suggests what it could be. Specifically, the book scrutinizes the media, which preeminently provide Western societies with the information and the tools to decide on the ways to address the problem. Given terrorism's unique dependence on publicity and amplification, the media have a crucial role in either facilitating or obstructing the spread of terrorism against the West.

Having defined the problem, examined its wellsprings, identified its catalysts, and observed its corrosive effects on the democracies, the book presents a strategy with which the West can wage successful war against terrorism. Since the Western democracies are societies rooted in law, the first requirement is to establish the legal foundations for waging the war. These are the legal principles, and the moral concepts from which they are derived, which in large measure are recognized throughout the West but need reaffirmation and clarification in the age of terror.

The book then proposes a two-front campaign against terrorism: a domestic battle, which the democracies can effectively prosecute by treating terrorism as a variant of organized crime, and a global battle, which requires above all a realignment of political attitudes in the West. The book draws on the successful examples of countries which have curbed the most violent terrorism or virtually stamped it out to demonstrate its fundamental message: that a policy of principle and firmness, applied consistently by the leading democracies, can stop the forces of world terror in their tracks and root out this malignancy from our civilization.

I

THE CHALLENGE TO
THE DEMOCRACIES

WHY IS THE WEST the target of terrorism? Spiritually, its values
are the direct antitheses of those of terrorism. In the democracies, legitimacy is derived from the consent of the governed;
even then, the government's power is limited by the strict obser-
vances of fundamental human freedoms, and conflicts are resolved by political, that is, non-violent, means.

But for the terrorist, there are no such restraints on either
legitimacy or power. Legitimacy is derived from whatever cause
he is fighting for or professes to be fighting for. There is no need
to ask the people. He, the terrorist, is the self-appointed arbiter
of what is just and necessary. If others do not quite see it that
way, they will be forced to submit to the terrorist's will by a
fearful violence that knows no limits and which claims everyone
and everything as a legitimate target.

But it is not only the clash of its humanity with terrorism's
inhumanity that has made the West terrorism's chief target.
There is another reason. Terrorists and their supporters view
the West as uniquely vulnerable to their attacks. They know
that the openness of Western societies affords them many
possibilities for attack. And they assume that the West's hu-
maneness and its emphasis on rule of law will inhibit a powerful
response. In particular, they rely on deniability. Very often
they will claim that someone else is responsible—some other

government, some other group, some other faction. With such protestations of innocence, the terrorists hope to escape punishment. They assume that if the democracies cannot affix blame, they will not act.

But in many cases, of course, it is perfectly possible to determine who the terrorists are and who stands behind them. If governments have failed to do this, it is more often not for lack of knowledge but for lack of courage and moral clarity. Some have sought to purchase immunity by striking deals with the terrorists. None of these deals has held up; those who entered into them emerged humiliated and weakened. Others have shied away from confronting terrorism by arguing that a firm response would engender more terrorism and is therefore morally and politically unacceptable.

Terrorism has thrived on such weakness and disunity. In a brief span of two decades, it has become a world force; it has attacked virtually every democracy; it threatens international travel, international commerce, international agreements. It can threaten much more tomorrow.

The West can and must defeat the forces of terror before they spread further. It must unite and fight to win the war against terrorism. This is the challenge facing the democracies, and the democracies alone can meet it.

Defining Terrorism

BENJAMIN NETANYAHU

THE WORLD periodically experiences fresh, and well-publicized, spasms of terrorism. For all the millions of words, the hundreds of hours of television time, the legions of experts, there is surprisingly little clarity. What is terrorism in the first place? Is it not really a term that we use to condemn acts of violence with which we happen to disagree? Are these acts isolated incidents, or are they somehow related to one another? Do they pose a fundamental threat to our society, or are they merely sensational news stories? Are they "senseless" killings, or do they have a purpose? Will they intensify or recede? Above all, what can we do about them; in fact, can *anything* be done?

In trying to understand international terrorism, we must first recognize that it is not a sporadic phenomenon born of social misery and frustration. It is rooted in the political ambitions and designs of expansionist states and the groups that serve them. Without the support of such states, *international* terrorism would be impossible. Compared to these governmental forces, the individual terrorists shrink into insignificance; whatever their motives, they could find no effective expression and their actions would have no lasting impact. The attempts to explain away terrorist outrages as the result of the "desperation" of individuals or groups are not only based on a simplistic fallacy; they neatly echo the terrorists' own assertions, which are meant to legitimize their criminal actions and divert public attention from the real forces behind terrorism. Such manipulation of public opinion is, in fact, central to the terrorist strategy. For this purpose, access to the media, indeed their domination, is indispensable.

And the media, as many journalists realize, have unwittingly played into the terrorists' hands. Newsmen, and their audiences, are mesmerized by the spectacle of it all. First the terrorists seize our attention by committing a brutal act. Only then does the real performance begin: the communiqués, the parading of dazed hostages before the cameras, the endless interviews in which the terrorists are respectfully asked to explain their demands and conditions and, more significantly, the *reasons* for their actions.

Slowly, imperceptibly, the initial horror recedes, and in its place comes a readiness to accept the terrorists' point of view. We in the West, after all, are accustomed to believe that there is always another "point of view" worth looking at, even when it comes to terrorists. Before we know it, the hijackers and killers have spokesmen and commentators of their own, and the terrorists have been transformed into merely another type of political activist, with a grievance that has to be "considered," even given equal time.

We are asked to shed our normal revulsion for murderous acts and accept the notion, endlessly repeated, that "one man's terrorist is another man's freedom fighter." This is precisely what the terrorists would like us to believe. The ease with which they and their sympathizers succeed in imposing this false symmetry into our language is rooted in our failure to come to grips with the essence of terrorism. Most people, of course, instinctively recognize one distinct aspect of terrorism when they see it—violence directed against persons who have no connection with the alleged grievance the terrorist purports to remedy. When an Air India airplane is blown up in midair or when American passengers are "executed" in the Middle East, no one has any doubt that these are terrorist acts. What do the American passengers of TWA have to do with the Shiites? What do the Canadian passengers of Air India have to do with the Sikhs?

Obviously, anyone with an inkling of moral feeling would consider attacks on such targets outrageous. But not the terrorist.

He chooses innocent victims precisely because they *are* innocent. By attacking them, he willfully breaks down the limits of
acceptable conflict and broadens it to include anyone, especially
victims chosen at random. By such actions, the terrorist tells
the world that he will go to any lengths to achieve his purpose,
which is to make governments cave in to his demands.

Yet some assert that any act of war resulting in civilian deaths
is a kind of terrorism. An incident from World War II demonstrates the absurdity of this contention. In 1944 the RAF set out
to bomb Gestapo headquarters in Copenhagen. The bombers,
however, missed and instead hit a hospital, killing scores of
children. This was a tragic accident of war. But in no sense can
it be called terrorism. What distinguishes terrorism is the *willful
and calculated* choice of innocents as targets. When terrorists
machine-gun a passenger waiting area or set off bombs in a
crowded shopping center, their victims are not accidents of war
but the *very objects* of the terrorists' assault.

I am prepared, at the risk of belaboring the point, to offer a
formal definition, the one adopted in Jerusalem in 1979: *Terrorism is the deliberate and systematic murder, maiming, and
menacing of the innocent to inspire fear for political ends*. This
distinction is no mere quibble, but lies at the heart of the problem. For without a clear understanding of terrorism, the problem
cannot be tackled.

The word "deliberate" distinguishes terrorist victims from the
accidental civilian casualties in every war; the word "systematic"
indicates that terrorism is not an aberration but a methodical
campaign of repeated outrages. The violation is the norm.

It is with the clear intention of blurring these distinctions that
the terrorists habitually describe themselves as "guerrillas." And
the media uncritically adopt their terminology. But guerrillas
are not terrorists. They are irregular soldiers who wage war on
regular military forces, not on civilians. (The term was first used
by the Spaniards in 1810 for the makeshift units they formed to
fight Napoleon's army.) Actually, guerrillas are the very opposite
of terrorists. While they pit themselves against far-superior *combatants*, terrorists choose to attack weak and defenseless *civilians*: old men, women, children—anyone in fact *except* soldiers,

if they can avoid it. Civilians, then, are the key to the terrorists' strategy. They kill civilians, and more often than not, they hide behind them—hoping that the prospect of more innocent deaths will help them escape retribution.

This indeed is terrorism's most pernicious effect: it blurs the distinction between combatants and non-combatants, the central tenet of the laws of war. There are those who say that war is war, and that any attempt to define ethical limits to war is futile. But short of the rare and difficult case of total war, such as during the last world war, when the Allies took up the tactic of bombing German cities after the Nazis had begun the practice by bombing Dutch and British cities, most people would agree that there is a significant difference between waging war on armed combatants and attacking defenseless civilians. Without this distinction, the concept of war crimes loses any meaning. For if everything is permissible, why *not* gas innocent people or machine-gun schoolchildren?

It is here where the terrorist parts company with humanity. *He declares a total war on the society he attacks.* For him everyone is a legitimate target. A baby is fair game; he may, after all, grow up to be a soldier. So is the baby's mother; she gave birth to this future soldier. No one is spared, ordinary citizens and leaders alike. For in addition to random killing, terrorists often engage in assassinations of a society's leaders, as in the murder of Italian Premier Aldo Moro or the attempted assassination of the Pope. Assassination, in fact, is important to the genesis of modern terrorism, emerging from an older tradition that maintains that a society can be reshaped, or a creed cleansed, by eliminating its leaders or ruling class. But in the case of modern revolutionaries, it soon became apparent that they seldom bothered to define where such a class ends. It could extend from the ruler to his functionaries, to sympathizers and abettors, to class enemies and corrupters of the faith, to counterrevolutionaries and infidels—in short, to anyone. For the terrorist, assassination is the precursor of mass murder, and both constitute the principal weapons in his arsenal. Random or selective, the principle is always the same. The targets are innocent civilians whom no one, except the terrorist, would conceivably classify as combatants.

Having defined all of society as a field of combat, the terrorist demands that his activity, which would ordinarily be viewed as gangsterism, be treated with the respect given to legitimate warfare. That is why he often takes on all the trappings of a soldier; that is why he issues "communiqués" instead of simple statements; and why he insists that his jailed accomplices, who are in fact dangerous criminals, be accorded the status of prisoners of war.

Thus, in its choice of targets and its demands for legitimacy, terrorism breaks down the pivotal distinctions that define the moral limits of war. It takes us back to the impulses of a savage era before society submitted to the rule of law. Therein lies the first and greatest danger it poses to our civilization.

Though terrorism as such is not new in history, or even in this century, today's terrorism radically differs from earlier forms of terrorism in its frequency and the extent of its violence; it now attacks the territory and nationals of nearly all the democracies. How did this situation come about? What are the forces behind it?

Terrorism began its rapid growth in the 1960s. It was sparked by the early successes of two groups of terrorists: the PLO, which introduced airline hijacking as an international weapon, and European radical factions which carried out increasingly bold bombings, kidnappings, and assassinations throughout the Continent. Terrorist groups, seemingly independent from one another, soon proliferated throughout Europe, Japan, North and South America, and the Middle East. But as the evidence piled up, the Arab PLO, the Iranian Mujahdeen, the Armenian ASALA, the German Baader-Meinhof gang, the Italian Red Brigades, the Japanese Red Army, and others were often found to be linked not only to one another but to the Soviet Union and radical Arab regimes as well. Only after the PLO's expulsion from Beirut did captured PLO documents reveal the pivotal role of its terrorist mini-state in Lebanon as a training center and launching ground for what had become a kind of terrorist international.

This collaboration between Marxist and Muslim radicals is not accidental. Modern terrorism has its roots in two movements that have assumed international prominence in the second half of the twentieth century, communist totalitarianism and Islamic (and Arab) radicalism. These forces have given terrorism its ideological impetus and much of its material support. Both legitimize unbridled violence in the name of a higher cause, both are profoundly hostile to democracy, and both have found in terrorism an ideal weapon for waging war against it. And each has given rise to organizations which put these principles to work.

But these terrorist organizations would not have gotten very far had they not been actively supported by states that were built on the foundations of Marxism and radical Islam. Indeed, international terrorism is overwhelmingly an extension of warfare sustained and supported by these states. The Soviet Union, several of its Eastern European satellites, Cuba and North Korea on the one hand, and Middle Eastern states such as Libya, Iran, Syria, Iraq, and South Yemen on the other, have given terrorists weapons, training, and money. They have also provided sanctuary, safe passage, and safe houses, often using their embassies and diplomatic pouches for these purposes. But this assistance to terrorism is not limited to the operational plane. It is also given on the crucial political level, especially in the campaign to legitimize terrorism and to block international measures against it.

The typical stratagem at the United Nations, for example, has been to justify terrorism by calling it a struggle for national liberation. This is perverse enough in itself, because terrorism is always unjustifiable, regardless of its professed or real goals. But it is perverse in another way. For the real goals of terrorists *are* in practice related to their methods. History has repeatedly given us advance warning. Those who deliberately butcher women and children do not have liberation in mind. It is not only that the ends of terrorists do not justify the means they choose. It is that the choice of means indicates what the true ends are. Far from being fighters for freedom, terrorists are the forerunners of tyranny. It is instructive to note that the French Resistance did not resort to the systematic killing of German women and children, well within reach in occupied France. A few years later, in Algeria, the FLN showed no such restraint against the French occupation. France, of course, is today a democracy,

Algeria merely another of the many despotisms where terrorists have come to power. Similarly, the PLO was established years *before* a single Israeli soldier stood in the area it now purportedly wants to liberate; the PLO's charter clearly states its goal: to liquidate Israel. Yet the slogan of national liberation, blithely uttered by the Soviet and Arab blocs and uncritically accepted by many in the West, has been remarkably successful in legitimizing terrorism and neutralizing opposition to it.

Without the support offered by the Soviet bloc and the Arab world, international terrorism would revert to its earlier, localized manifestations before the 1960s and would hardly dominate the global scene. To see what a difference state support makes, consider the political loyalities of today's better-known and successful terrorists. Virtually all are left-wing and Middle Eastern extremists. It is not that terrorists or other political affiliations do not exist. They do. A few groups of right-wing terrorists can be found, mostly in Latin America, some in Italy and France. Their hostility to democracy is just as adamant as that of their left-wing counterparts. Like them, they are offshoots (in this case, remnants) of totalitarianism, this time of the fascist variety that threatened democracy in the 1930s. But there the similarity ends. For unlike the left, their state sponsors are virtually nonexistent. Without governments to offer them intelligence, funds, embassies, and the like, their size and effectiveness are insignificant.

Why have states begun to resort to terrorism? Since the end of World War II and the dawn of the nuclear age, the waging of war has become increasingly risky. For a superpower like the Soviet Union, a direct confrontation with the West entails the unacceptable risks of atomic war. For smaller states, conventional war can also escalate into intolerable conflict, or outright defeat. Terrorism is part of the broader trend toward war by proxy. It permits regimes to engage in aggression while evading retaliation. Nasser, for example, established the PLO in Cairo in 1964 as a means of destabilizing Jordan, and, equally, for continuing his unsuccessful war against Israel.

Foreign governments do not necessarily *create* the domestic conflicts that provide the background to indigenous terrorism.

These can have many origins, such as ethnic, class, religious, ideological, sectarian, and irredentist clashes. But in nearly all instances, when a terrorist group survives and grows, it will sooner or later receive outside support. Terrorism is simply too tempting a weapon to be forsaken. When we see, therefore, an enduring campaign of terrorism in a country, it is not too far-fetched to suspect state involvement. I do not refer, of course, to internal state terror, a practice made infinitely more horrible in this century by the Russian and Chinese revolutions, and by Nazism. I mean the involvement of *foreign* governments in assisting terrorist groups to subvert or topple the home regime. Again, that is the distinguishing feature of terrorism in our time.

And as the number of attacks has increased tenfold in the last decade alone, a clear pattern has emerged. The targets of terrorism have been, more and more, Britain and Germany, Spain and Portugal, France and Italy, Israel and Japan, and, above all, the United States (whose nationals accounted for roughly a third of terrorism's victims since 1968)—in short, the West. The liberal democracies of Europe and North America, the handful of democracies in Asia, and their non-radical allies in the Middle East, Latin America, and the South Pacific, are everywhere under assault. A network of professional terrorists seeks to weaken and demoralize democratic societies by attacking their citizens, their leaders, their institutions, thereby disrupting their way of life and sapping their political will.

And it is a growing threat. Terrorist attacks now kill and injure not one or two, but hundreds at a time. Few can doubt that other, more lethal weapons would be employed. The spread of lawlessness and the blatant disregard of any constraints by governments are, as in the thirties, gradually becoming accepted norms again, and the consequences could be intolerable. By far the most disconcerting prospect would be acquisition of weapons of mass destruction by the principal terrorist states of the Middle East—Iran, Libya, and Syria. These regimes pose a much greater threat to their neighbors, and to the democratic world generally, than has yet been acknowledged.

The democracies have by and large failed to meet the terrorist challenge. They have failed to recognize the far-reaching effects unbridled terrorism will have on their security and have stood divided rather than united. They cannot afford to do so any longer.

The Challenge to the Democracies

GEORGE P. SHULTZ

IN RECENT YEARS the world has seen two major developments: one a cause for great distress, the other a reason for hope. The distressing fact is that terrorism has been increasing. Significantly more people are being killed or injured by international terrorists than in the late 1960s, when governments began keeping records.

Even more alarming has been the rise of terrorism sponsored by states. Many countries have joined the ranks of what we might call the "League of Terror" as full-fledged sponsors and supporters of indiscriminate, and not so indiscriminate, murder. Terrorist attacks backed by what Qaddafi calls the "holy alliance" of Libya, Syria, and Iran, and attacks launched by North Korea and others have taken a heavy toll of innocent lives. As a result, more of the world's people must today live in fear of sudden and unprovoked violence at the hands of terrorists. The epidemic is spreading, and the civilized world is still groping for remedies.

Nevertheless, there is also cause for hope. Thanks in large measure to the efforts of concerned governments and private organizations like the Jonathan Institute, the peoples of the free world have finally begun to grapple with the problem of terrorism, in intellectual and in practical terms. I say intellectual because the first step toward a solution to any problem is to understand that there *is* a problem, and then to understand its nature. In recent years we have learned a great deal about terrorism, though our education has been painful and costly. We know what kind of threat international terrorism poses to our free society. We have learned much about the terrorists themselves, their backers, their targets, their diverse methods, their underlying motives, and their eventual goals. Armed with this knowledge, we can focus our energies on the practical means for reducing and eventually eliminating the threat.

What we have learned about terrorism is, first, that it is not random, undirected, purposeless violence. It is not, like an earthquake or a hurricane, an act of nature before which we are helpless. Terrorists and those who support them have definite goals; terrorist violence is the means of attaining those goals. Our response must be twofold: We must deny them the means, but above all we must deny them their goals.

But what are the goals of terrorism? We know that terrorists use a variety of methods, resources, instruments, and that they can have many *immediate* aims. Terrorists may range from the lone individual who plants a homemade bomb in a shopping center, to the small clandestine group that kidnaps and assassinates public figures, to the well-equipped and well-financed organization that uses unbridled violence to terrorize an entire population. Their *stated* objectives may range from separatist causes, to revenge for ethnic grievances, to social and political revolution. It is clear that our response will have to fit the precise character and circumstances of the specific threats.

But we must understand that the overarching goal of all terrorists is the same. With rare exceptions, they are attempting to impose their will by force, a special kind of force designed to create an atmosphere of fear. And their efforts are directed at destroying what we are seeking to build.

The United States and its democratic allies are morally committed to certain ideals and to a humane vision of the future. In our foreign policies, we try to foster the kind of world that promotes peaceful settlement of disputes, one that welcomes change without violent conflict. We seek a world in which human rights are respected by all governments, one based on the rule of law. We know that in a global community where *all* nations share these blessings, our own democracy will flourish, our own nation will prosper, and our own people will continue to enjoy freedom.

Nor has ours been a fruitless search. In our lifetime we have seen the world progress, though perhaps too slowly, toward this goal. Civilized norms of conduct have evolved, even governing relations between adversaries. Conflict persists, but with some notorious exceptions, even wars have been conducted within certain restraints. Indiscriminate slaughter of innocents is widely condemned, and the use of certain kinds of weapons has been proscribed; most nations have heeded those proscriptions.

We all know that the world as it exists is still far from our ideal vision. But today even the progress that mankind has already made is endangered by those who do not share that vision—indeed, who violently oppose it.

For we must understand, above all, that terrorism is a form of *political* violence. Wherever it takes place, it is directed in an important sense against *us*, the democracies, against our most basic values and often our fundamental strategic interests. The values upon which democracy is based—individual rights, equality under the law, freedom of thought and expression, and freedom of religion—all stand in the way of those who seek to impose their ideologies or their religious beliefs by force. A terrorist has no patience and no respect for the orderly processes of democratic society and, therefore, he considers himself its enemy.

The very qualities that make democracies so hateful to the terrorists also make them so vulnerable. Precisely because we maintain the most open societies, terrorists have unparalleled opportunity to strike against us.

The antagonism between democracy and terrorism seems so basic that it is hard to understand why so much intellectual confusion still exists on the subject. We have all heard the insidious claim that "one man's terrorist is another man's freedom fighter." The great American Senator Henry Jackson rebutted this notion at the Jonathan Institute's 1979 conference:

> The idea that one person's "terrorist" is another's "freedom fighter" cannot be sanctioned. Freedom fighters or revolutionaries don't blow up buses containing non-combatants; terrorist murderers do. Freedom fighters don't set out to capture and slaughter school-

children; terrorist murderers do. Freedom fighters don't assassinate innocent businessmen, or hijack and hold hostage innocent men, women, and children; terrorist murderers do. It is a disgrace that democracies would allow the treasured word "freedom" to be associated with acts of terrorists.

Where democracy is struggling to take root, the terrorist is its enemy. He seeks to spread chaos and disorder, to paralyze a society. In doing so, he wins no converts to his cause; his deeds inspire hatred and fear, not allegiance. The terrorist seeks to undermine institutions, to destroy popular faith in moderate government, and to shake the people's belief in the very idea of democracy. In Lebanon, for example, state-sponsored terrorism has exploited existing tensions and prevented that nation from rebuilding its democratic institutions.

Where the terrorist cannot bring about anarchy, he may try to force the government to overreact, or to impose tyrannical measures of control, and hence lose the support of the people. Turkey faced such a challenge. Martial law was imposed, the terrorist threat was drastically reduced, and today we see democracy returning to that country. In Argentina, the widely and properly deplored "disappearances" of the late 1970s were, in fact, part of a response—a deliberately provoked response—to a massive campaign of terrorism. Other countries around the world face similar challenges, and they, too, must steer their course carefully between anarchy and tyranny. The lesson for civilized nations is that we must respond to the terrorist threat within the rule of law, lest we become unwitting accomplices in the terrorist's scheme to undermine civilized society.

Once we understand terrorism's goals and methods, it is not hard to tell, as we look around the world, who are the terrorists and who are the freedom fighters. The resistance fighters in Afghanistan do not destroy villages or kill the helpless. The Contras in Nicaragua do not blow up school buses or hold mass executions of civilians.

How tragic it would be if democratic societies so lost confidence in their own moral legitimacy that they lost sight of the obvious: that violence directed against democracy or the hopes for democracy lacks fundamental justification. Democracy offers mechanisms for peaceful change, legitimate political competition, and redress of grievances. Resort to arms in behalf of democracy against repressive regimes or movements is, indeed, a fight for freedom, since there may be no other way that freedom can be achieved.

What the free nations cannot afford is to let the uncritical corruption of language hamper our efforts to defend ourselves, our interests, or our friends. We know the difference between terrorists and freedom fighters, and our policies reflect that distinction. Those who strive for freedom and democracy will always have the sympathy and, when possible, the support of the American people. We will oppose guerrilla wars whenever they threaten to spread totalitarian rule or deny the rights of national independence and self-determination. But we will oppose terrorism no matter what banner it may fly. For terrorism in the service of *any* cause is the enemy of freedom.

If freedom and democracy are the targets of terrorism, it is clear that totalitarianism is its ally. The number of terrorist incidents in or against totalitarian states is negligible. States that support and sponsor terrorist actions have managed in recent years to coopt and manipulate terrorist groups in pursuit of their own strategic goals. It is not by chance that most acts of terrorism occur in areas of importance to the West. More than three-quarters of the world's terrorist attacks in 1983 occurred in Western Europe, Latin America, and the Middle East. As the Joint Chiefs of Staff have said: "Terrorists may or may not be centrally controlled by their patrons. Regardless, the instability they create in the industrialized West and Third World nations undermines the security interests of the United States and its allies."

States that sponsor terrorism are using it as another weapon of warfare, to gain strategic advantage where they cannot use conventional means. When Iran and its allies sent terrorists to bomb Western personnel in Beirut, they hoped to weaken the West's commitment to defending its interests in the Middle East. When North Korea sponsored the murder of South Korean government officials, it hoped to weaken the non-communist stronghold on the mainland of East Asia. The terrorists who assault Israel are also enemies of the United States. When Libya and the PLO provide arms and training to the communists of Central America, they are aiding Soviet efforts to undermine our security in that vital region. When the Soviet Union and its clients provide financial, logistic, and training support for terrorists worldwide; when the Red Brigades in Italy and the Red Army Faction in Germany assault free countries in the name of communist ideology—they hope to shake the West's self-confidence and sap its will to resist aggression and intimidation.

We should understand the Soviet role in international terrorism without exaggeration or distortion. The Soviet Union officially denounces the use of terrorism as an instrument of state policy. Yet there is a wide gap between Soviet words and Soviet actions. One does not have to believe that the Soviets are puppeteers and the terrorists marionettes; violent or fanatic individuals and groups are indigenous to every society. But in many countries, terrorism would long since have passed away had it not been for significant support from outside. The international links among terrorist groups are now clearly understood; and the Soviet link, direct or indirect, is also understood. The Soviets use terrorist groups for their own purposes, and *their* goal is always the same: to weaken liberal democracy and undermine world stability.

Having identified the challenge, we must now consider the best strategy to counter it. We must keep in mind, as we devise our strategy, that our ultimate aim is to preserve what the terrorists seek to destroy: democracy, freedom, and the hope for a world at peace.

The battle against terrorism must begin at home. Terrorism has no place in our society. We have taken vigorous steps to see that it is not imported from abroad.* The FBI is improving our ability to detect and prevent terrorist acts within our own borders. We must also ensure that our people and facilities in other countries are better protected against terrorist attacks. We are strengthening security at our embassies around the world to try

---

* We have enacted legislation to offer rewards for information about terrorists, and have already employed this new authority on several occasions.

to prevent a recurrence of the Beirut and Kuwait embassy bombings.

While we take these measures to protect our own citizens, we know that terrorism is an international problem that requires the concerted efforts of all free nations. Just as there is collaboration among those who engage in terrorism, so there must be cooperation among those who are its actual and potential targets. An essential component of our strategy, therefore, is greater cooperation among the democratic nations and all others who share our hopes for the future. We have achieved some successes. But too often countries are inhibited by fear of losing commercial opportunities or fear of provoking the bully. The time has come for the nations that truly seek an end to terrorism to join together, in whatever forums, to take the necessary steps.

Greater international cooperation offers many advantages. If we can collectively improve our gathering and sharing of intelligence, we can better detect the movements of terrorists, anticipate their actions, and bring them to justice. We can also help provide the training and share the knowledge of antiterrorist tactics.*

We must also make a collective effort to address the special problem of state-sponsored terrorism. States that support terrorism offer them safe havens, funds, training, and logistical support. We must find ways to pressure members of the League of Terror to cease their support. Such pressure will have to be international, for no one country can exert enough influence alone. Economic sanctions and other forms of pressure impose costs on the nation that applies them, but some sacrifices will be necessary if we are to solve the problem. In the long run, it will have been a small price to pay.

We must also discourage nations from paying blackmail to terrorist organizations. Although we recognize that some nations are particularly vulnerable to the terrorist threat, we must con-

---

* The American government has trained foreign law-enforcement officers in anti-terrorist techniques, and implemented two international conventions to which the United States is a party: the International Convention Against the Taking of Hostages and the Montreal Convention, which protects against sabotage of civilian aircraft and air navigation facilities.

vince them that paying tribute is counterproductive and inimical to the interests of all.

Finally, the nations of the free world must stand together against terrorism to demonstrate our enduring commitment to our shared vision. The terrorists may be looking for signs of weakness, for evidence of disunity. We must show them that we are unbending. Let the terrorists despair of ever achieving their goals.

All the measures I have described so far, domestic and international, are important elements in a comprehensive strategy. But are they enough? Is the purely passive defense that these measures represent sufficient to cope with the problem? Can we as a country, can the community of free nations, stand in a purely defensive posture and absorb the blows dealt by terrorists?

I think not. From a practical standpoint, a purely passive defense does not provide enough of a deterrent to terrorism and the states that sponsor it. It is time to think long, hard, and seriously about more active means of defense—defense through appropriate preventive or preemptive actions against terrorist groups *before* they strike.

We will need to strengthen our capabilities in the area of intelligence and quick reaction. Intelligence will be particularly important, since our societies demand that we know with reasonable clarity just what we are doing and against whom we are acting. Experience has taught us that one of the best deterrents to terrorism is the certainty that swift and sure measures will be taken against those who engage in it. As President Reagan has said:

> We must make it clear to any country that is tempted to use violence to undermine democratic governments, destabilize our friends, thwart efforts to promote democratic governments, or disrupt our lives, that it has nothing to gain, and much to lose.

Clearly there are complicated moral issues here. But there should be no doubt of the democracies' moral right, indeed duty, to defend themselves. And there should be no doubt of the profound issue at stake. The democracies seek a world order that is based on justice. When innocents are victimized and the guilty go unpunished, the terrorists have succeeded in undermining the very foundation of civilized society, for they have created a world where there is no justice. This is a blow to our most fundamental moral values and a dark cloud over the future of humanity. We can do better than this.

No matter what strategy we pursue, the terrorist threat will not disappear overnight. We must understand this and be prepared to live with the fact that despite all our best efforts the world is still a dangerous place. Further sacrifices, as in the past, may be the price we will have to pay for preserving our freedom.

It is essential, therefore, that we not allow the actions of terrorists to affect our policies or deflect us from our goals. When terrorism succeeds in intimidating governments into altering their foreign policies, it only opens the door to more terrorism. It shows that terrorism works; it emboldens those who resort to it, and it encourages others to join their ranks.

But if we remain firm, we can look ahead to a time when terrorism will cease to be a major factor in world affairs. We must face that challenge with realism, determination, and strength of will. I have great faith that we do have such will, and the capability to act decisively against this threat. It is really up to us, the nations of the free world. We must apply ourselves to the task of ensuring our future and consigning terrorism to its own dismal past.

Terrorists and Freedom Fighters

BENZION NETANYAHU

ANY ATTEMPT to address the problem of terrorism entails a grave responsibility. For in discussing terrorism, we seek to determine the stand we should take in a hard and crucial struggle which touches not only on our current security but also on the worth of our future lives. Indeed, as I see it, what is involved is nothing less than the survival of free society itself.

Several years ago, few in the West realized all the implications of terrorism. Now there are many in the free societies who recognize its essence and what it entails. Today we see leaders of the free world, especially the leading statesmen of America, approaching the front lines of this battle and seeking ways to put a halt to the blight. This is certainly a heartening development whose importance cannot be overestimated.

At the same time, however, we see leaders in the West, and many in the press and the public at large, who are still hesitant about the stand they should take toward terrorism and those who fight it. Still others believe that the proper course to follow is one of political accommodation with the terrorists, though admittedly they are not at all sure that such an accommodation is feasible.

Both these attitudes are extremely harmful, since both prevent the West from closing ranks and forming a common and united front, which alone can cope with the terrorist menace. We certainly would like the doubters and accommodationists to join the advocates of active resistance. But before we can expect to convince them to do so, we must comprehend the motives and arguments of those who refuse to take a clear stand against terrorism, let alone meet it head-on.

Some maintain that this position derives from the immediate advantages, political or economic, which the statesmen concerned hope to reap for their countries from a compromise with the terrorists. That such considerations play a part in this matter is indeed hard to deny; yet it is equally hard to conceive that they alone determine such attitudes. It is not easy to assume that Western statesmen, whose patriotism must be held above question, would agree to ignore long-term dangers in exchange for short-term gains. It is more likely that the indecision of some statesmen, and the readiness of others to bend toward the terrorists, stems partly from confusion about the true nature of terrorism, and partly from a belief that the terrorists have a case—perhaps a just case—and that they can be reasoned with and finally won over by adequate concessions. *Realpolitik* is surely there, but behind it there is a *moral* consideration which is based on a misconception of terrorism and what the terrorists are after.

This misconception must be cleared up if we are to make any headway against terrorism. In doing so, we must bear in mind that we are dealing here with a crafty, potent enemy who operates not only with physical but also with psychological weapons, with persuasive arguments and captivating slogans. Thus, to delude the peoples of the free world, the terrorist appears as the bearer of *their* ideals, as the champion of the oppressed, as the critic of social ills, and, more specifically, as a fighter for freedom. The last claim, especially, is the sure catch which springs the trap for the credulous. Since freedom fighters have also used violence in their struggles, and since freedom is so dear to free men, many in the democracies are almost automatically filled with sympathy for the terrorists and their causes. Some young people in the West are even moved to join their ranks. Others, more observant, more critical, ask: *Who* are these men? Are they really freedom fighters as they claim to be, or are they merely using a pretense, a ruse, a guise under which they hide their real face—the face of quite another type of fighter and another type of man?

To answer these questions, we must first determine the nature of modern terrorism and how it relates to what is generally known as the struggle for human freedom. Terrorism was defined (in the 1979 Jonathan Institute conference on terrorism) as "the deliberate and systematic murder, maiming, and menacing of the innocent to inspire fear for political ends." This, we believe, is a correct definition, and it should have been sufficient for our purposes. But what definition, however perfect, cannot be submerged, evaded, or distorted by a campaign of shrewd demagogues proclaiming gross untruths from all the major forums of the world?

We should, therefore, sharpen that definition. More stress must be placed on the word "innocent," which, when properly underscored, cannot fail to expose the sham of the terrorist claims. For in contrast to the terrorist, no freedom fighter has ever deliberately attacked innocents. He has never deliberately killed small children, or passersby in the street, or foreign visitors, or other civilians who happen to reside in the area of conflict or are merely associated ethnically or religiously with the people of that area. This was not just a matter of tactics but one that related to his basic aim. For this aim, proclaimed in his title, implied the following simple syllogism: *To fight for freedom means to fight against oppression; oppression means violation of man's rights; hence to fight for freedom means to oppose such violations*. Consequently, no freedom fighter could stand for these violations, let alone perpetrate them himself.

Yet that is precisely what the terrorist does—and that in the most brazen and brutal manner. Hence he is not what he claims to be. Since he tramples underfoot all the rights of man, he cannot be regarded, by any stretch of logic, as a fighter for freedom. But then what is he? What is he fighting for?

It may be argued that he fights for the liberation of his own people, for *their* inherent rights, without regard for the rest of the world. This notion is belied by the actual record of the terrorists' conduct. The PLO, for instance, claims to be the "sole representative of the Palestinian people." We shall not examine here the merits of this claim. But nobody can deny that there has been *opposition* to the PLO among the Arabs, and no one who stands for man's basic freedoms can question the right of that opposition to its opinion. Does the PLO respect this right? The answer is given by the many Arabs who were cruelly liquidated by PLO killers for having merely expressed disagreement with their views, or were just suspected of such disagreement. And what about the right of free thought and expression *within* the ranks of the PLO itself? There, too, differences of opinion are settled by the assassin's bomb and gun. Remember how the terrorists in Lebanon fought each other to death over "questions of policy," as they put it. And remember the case of the PLO dissident Issam Sartawi, who advocated coexistence with Israel and was assassinated by PLO gunmen.

Of course it will be said that all this is unavoidable, that it is part and parcel of the "mechanics of revolution," which is allegedly the necessary *means* of liberation. Let us then consider the promise of free life the terrorist holds out for his "liberated" people *after* the "revolution." We can judge that promise by the performance of regimes in countries where the terrorists have prevailed. Look at Angola, at Libya, at Vietnam; look at Cambodia, at Cuba, at Iran—is there freedom there or despotic rule which employs all forms of oppression? The subjugated populations of these countries are so terrified by their ruling "liberators" that they do not even utter a whisper of protest against any of the abuses of their rights.

Yet some advocates of the terrorists still argue that it is better for a group to be subjugated by its own members than by members of a foreign people. When was this proven to be the rule? Oppression is oppression from whichever side it comes, and intolerable oppression remains intolerable even when practiced by your own kind. In fact, it is often far worse. When Mazzini, after Italy's liberation, was asked for his view about the possible establishment of a Marxist regime in Italy, he answered: "I would rather see the Austrians return to Italy than see the Italians slaves to themselves."

But we must also consider a third factor which shows clearly what the terrorist is. I refer to his patrons, promoters, and overlords, all of which are states with repressive regimes in which freedom has no place. The terrorists' connections with countries of the Middle East such as Syria, Libya, Iraq, and Iran are well known. These regimes have earned the title of terrorist states because they habitually use terror to further their aims. Not so well known, and often obscure, are the ties of the terrorists with the Soviet Union. And these are by far more important, more decisive, and more crucial for the future of the free world.

To be sure, the Soviets have repeatedly disclaimed their responsibility for the rise of terrorism in the world, but their deeds indisputably refute their denials. It is sufficient to note their treatment of the PLO, which has rightly been labeled the "core of world terror." They support them *politically* on an unprecedented scale. They support them *militarily* by offering them training in numerous bases within and outside the U.S.S.R. And they support them *legally* by preventing the effective implementation of an international convention for extraditing terrorists. There can be no doubt about the Soviets' motive. Terrorism is the first general attack upon a free society which the enemies of freedom plan to take over. When they succeed—that is, when the country attacked falls into the hands of the terrorist assailants—that country becomes a satellite of Soviet Russia and another launching ground for its political expansion.

The conclusion we must draw from all this is evident. Far from being a bearer of freedom, the terrorist is the carrier of oppression and enslavement. The three distinctive signs we have just mentioned—his method of warfare, which includes the murder of children; his oppressive rule over his own people; and his alliances with tyrannical regimes—indicate this unmistakably. If we point out these signs repeatedly, we should be able to destroy, as we must, the myth of the terrorist as a freedom fighter. But this is not enough. We should not only indicate what the terrorist is *not*; we must also show clearly what he *is*.

The terrorist represents a new breed of man which takes humanity back to prehistoric times, to the times when morality was not yet born. Divested of any moral principle, he has no moral sense, no moral controls, and is therefore capable of committing any crime, like a killing machine, without shame or remorse. But he is also a cunning, consummate liar, and therefore much more dangerous than the Nazis, who used to proclaim their aims openly. In fact, he is the perfect nihilist.

The harbingers of this type of man had already appeared a century ago, and then, too, they portrayed themselves as champions of "progress" and "true liberty," as the new wave of the approaching future. At that time, of course, it was difficult to see where all of this would lead. But a few great men did. One of these was Dostoevsky; another was Max Nordau. This is not the place, of course, to analyze the statements uttered by the heroes of Dostoevsky's novel *The Possessed*. But we can cite here Nordau's clear prognostications. Shocked by the sight of those terrible humans, and seeking to unmask them and reveal their aims, Nordau sounded the great alarm in his famous, and much misunderstood, *Degeneration*. "They are not the future," he cried, "but an immeasurably remote past. They are not progress, but the most appalling reaction. They are not liberty, but the most disgraceful slavery." Were their influence not destroyed, he added, the future would not bring the hoped-for brightness of day, but "the dusk of the nations, in which all suns and all stars gradually wane, and mankind with all its institutions and creations perishes in the midst of a dying world."

Today we can see that this was no apocalyptic vision but a forecast of a stark reality. Nordau did not speak of the death of mankind by nuclear destruction. The atomic bomb was then not yet envisioned. But civilizations may be subject to moral diseases which may destroy them as surely as any bomb can. Our attitude toward terrorism and the way we treat it, the way we are getting *conditioned* to its horrors, and, above all, our reactions to the dangers of enslavement represented by the terrorists and their masters—all these are symptoms of a serious moral sickness that debilitates our capacities to act as free men. And yet we feel within ourselves the power of recovery and the ability to emerge triumphant. May God grant us the wisdom to cure ourselves before the dusk of the nations is upon us.

The Cancer of Terrorism

PAUL JOHNSON

TERRORISM is the cancer of the modern world. No state is immune to it. It is a dynamic organism which attacks the healthy flesh of the surrounding society. It has the essential hallmark of malignant cancer: unless treated, and treated drastically, its growth is inexorable, until it poisons and engulfs the society on which it feeds and drags it down to destruction.

Modern terrorism dates from the middle 1960s, when the PLO formally adopted terror and mass murder as its primary policy. Terrorism was thus able to draw on the immense financial resources of the Arab oil states, and on the military training programs of the Soviet Union and of its satellites, Cuba, South Yemen, Vietnam, and North Korea. Over one thousand PLO killers have been trained in the Soviet Union alone. Moreover, from 1970 to 1982, the PLO operated a quasi-occupation of Lebanon, and was thus able to enjoy, in practice, all the advantages of its own sovereign territory. It acquired the weaponry of a sizable modern army and set up terrorist training camps of its own, used as facilities by the Red Brigades, the IRA, and a score of other killer gangs throughout the world.

This *physical* growth of the terrorist cancer was accompanied by a progressive elevation in its *moral* status. Yasir Arafat ceased to be a mere gangster leader and became, in effect, a terrorist statesman. He moved around the world with increasing diplomatic pomp, and was greeted on a level of moral equality by more and more world leaders. He and his organization finally achieved, at the United Nations, a position of privilege granted to no other body not a sovereign state. But perhaps his greatest moral triumph was to be received, and photographed being greeted, by the Pope—his Holiness and his Depravity together.

Inevitably, with the physical and moral growth of the terrorist international, came a growth in its *military* capacity. From the ability to kill individuals grew the ability to kill scores, then hundreds, now thousands. Not merely the PLO but its junior allies began to handle munitions on a prodigious scale. It is now common for the IRA, for instance, to stage killings involving two or three tons of high explosives. International terrorists operating in a score of countries now have the power to shoot down aircraft, destroy armored vehicles, and destroy heavily protected security posts. There is the danger, frighteningly obvious to all of us, that terrorists will eventually possess nuclear weapons, but a more immediate risk is that they will secure—perhaps already have secured—the devastating modern equipment now moving into the inventories of official armies: high-speed machine pistols firing 1,200 rounds a minute and almost soundless, lightweight grenade launchers and mortars, squirtless flamethrowers, short-range portable anti-tank weapons, shoulder-fired rocket launchers, and, most alarming of all, the new generation of portable missiles which have long ranges, are highly accurate, and can be carried and fired by one man or woman.

At whom will these devastating new weapons be aimed? The question is pointless. They are aimed at the world, at civilized society everywhere. They will be used to destroy not merely security forces but ordinary civilians: men, women, children. For, just as there seems to be no upper limit to the terrorist's arsenal, so there is no lowest depth beyond which the terrorist cannot sink in his moral declension. So ask not for whom the terrorist bell tolls: it tolls for thee, and thee, and thee—for decent, innocent people everywhere.

But in the growth of the terrorist cancer, a still more sinister aspect even than the expansion of its arsenals is the arrival of the first terrorist states. If Soviet Russia and four of its satellites actively train and arm terrorist movements, we now have the phenomenon of two regimes—Iran and Libya—which constitute terrorist states in themselves. These states do not merely finance, arm, and train foreign terrorists, providing them with bases and havens; they operate their own official machinery of international terrorism.

Both Iran and Libya now deploy, as part of their official armed forces and government machinery, assisted and provisioned by their embassies and diplomats, heavily armed, highly trained, and totally ruthless gangs of killers, who roam the world seeking out and destroying political or religious opponents—or mere critics—and in the process killing and maiming bystanders and destroying property throughout the West. These states conduct such policies of government terrorism while still enjoying all the privileges of sovereign status and all the protection of international law—membership in the United Nations and its agencies, access to the IMF, the World Bank, and the International Court, and the aegis of the Vienna and Hague Conventions.

Iran and Libya illustrate the extent to which the terrorist cancer has established its grip on the world's health, and our paralytic failure to treat the disease. Let me remind you of one of Iran's gigantic crimes of state terrorism: the seizure of all the occupants of the embassy of the United States, the greatest power on earth, as hostages. That crime goes unrepented and unpunished. Yet Iran still operates privileged embassies throughout the world to service its killers. It is still a member of the United Nations, where it can defend its policies of mass murder. It has been destroying the world's shipping in the Persian Gulf—maritime terrorism on a gigantic scale—or, to give it the old name, piracy. Will that go unpunished, too?

Or again, another example: one or more professional state terrorists, living in and working from the Libyan embassy in London, murdered a young British policewoman, in broad daylight and in front of hundreds of people. Under the protection of the Vienna Convention, on whose provision Colonel Qaddafi insisted down to the last comma, the killer or killers were allowed to leave Britain without search or investigation. Here was a murderous dictator who has sponsored terrorism all over the world, who operates his own terror squads, organizes and finances others, who has caused, extended, or prolonged no fewer than ten civil and interstate wars in Africa, who is responsible for the deaths of thousands, and who openly proclaims his contempt for international order; here he is able to take the maximum possible advantage of the conventions which govern behavior between law-abiding states.

Thus, with the emergence of the terrorist state, the cancer has spread to the point where it is multiplying its cells from within the framework of world order. The inmates are taking over the asylum; the doctors are helping to spread the bacillus. There is, then, no alternative to drastic treatment.

I have three propositions to put forward—the first on the *moral* level, the second on the *legal* level, the third on the *military* level. On the moral level, let us clear our minds of cant. By this I mean, let us reject the ambivalence with which civilized people often approach the problem of terrorism. They condemn terrorism in general and on principle, but there is often one particular group of terrorists which arouses their sympathy, for historical, racial, ethnic, or ideological reasons, and whom they are not prepared to describe as terrorists but rather as freedom fighters and guerrillas. One case is a small section of the Irish community in the United States and its sympathy for the IRA. The IRA is beyond question one of the most evil and destructive terrorist movements on earth. But it could not exist without the regular financial support it receives from some otherwise law-abiding and peaceful American-Irish.

I would counter this ambivalence in the civilized world by a simple proposition: There is no such person as a "good" terrorist, anywhere, at any time, in any circumstances. In fighting terrorism, there cannot be qualifications. Terrorism must be fought with the same absolute rigor with which the civilized powers once fought piracy and the international slave trade. There were no "good" pirates. There were no "good" slavers. There can be no "good" gunmen.

And let us note, at the same time, that the gunmen, the terrorists, do not, and by their nature cannot, achieve legitimate political aims. Under no circumstances can democratic societies be the beneficiaries of terrorism. The only gainers are anarchy

on the one hand and totalitarianism on the other, the twin Frank-
enstein monsters which threaten to overwhelm the democratic
West.

Let me give two illustrations of what I mean. What has the
PLO, the quintessential terrorist movement of modern times,
achieved? After the PLO and the other terrorist movements it
succored racked up an appalling total of lives extinguished and
property destroyed, how far have they progressed toward achieving their stated political ends? Not at all; in fact they have re-
gressed. The Palestinian state is further away than ever. The
Israeli state is stronger and more firmly established than in 1964,
when the PLO was founded. The PLO's victims have been the
Arab states which harbored the gunmen. Jordan saved itself in
1970 because it threw them out. Lebanon perished because it
lacked the courage to do the same. That is always the pattern:
If the only ultimate beneficiaries of terrorism are totalitarian
regimes, the chief victims are weak-minded democracies which
lack the perception and courage to treat terrorism as a mortal
enemy.

Again, take the IRA. They have killed over a thousand people,
most of them their own countrymen, since 1968. But the unitary
Irish state is as far away as ever, and they themselves constitute
the chief obstacle to its realization. Meanwhile, what has happened to the Irish Republic, which has throughout observed that
fatal ambivalence toward terrorism which I have described? The
very fabric of its state is under threat, and—since the IRA finances itself through the drug trade—Ireland now has one of
the biggest drug problems in Western Europe. No harm of any
consequence has been inflicted on Britain; it is Ireland and her
people who are the victims of the men with guns.

Now let us look briefly at the *legal* level. If there are no "good"
terrorists, it follows that civilized states must act collectively
against all of them. Of course, the United Nations is useless;
terrorist states are among its honored members. NATO is inappropriate. I put no faith in the European Anti-Terrorist Convention, even if everyone could be persuaded to sign it. Indeed,
I put no faith in any formal treaty arrangement—you end up
with a Vienna Convention. But I have a lot of faith in practical,

informal, and flexible arrangements between the major civilized powers.

We have to grasp the fact that to hurt one terrorist movement is to hurt them all. So, on the *military* level, I would like to see a coordinated, well-financed, informal, and secret effort by the major civilized powers to discover and exchange information about movements, routes, identities, weapons stocks, methods, plans, codes, safe houses, and bases of all terrorists everywhere. We must be prepared to devise and carry through concerted operations. The hydra is less likely to survive if struck simultaneously in several places. All the democracies must have their trained anti-terrorist units, and they must be accustomed to acting in concert.

For the terrorist, there can be no hiding places. The terrorist must never be allowed to feel safe anywhere in the world. He must be made to fear he is being followed, not just by agents of the government against which he is conspiring, but by the agents of many governments, coordinated by a common system. A terrorist kept constantly on the defensive is an ineffective terrorist.

No hiding places means that, sooner or later, the civilized powers must be prepared to act directly against the terrorist states. Looking back over the last two decades, we can claim some notable successes against individual terrorist movements. But these have been essentially defensive successes. Only on one occasion has a major offensive blow been dealt against the system of international terrorism itself. That was in 1982, when Israel crossed into Lebanon and expelled the PLO by force. By having had the moral and physical courage to violate a so-called sovereign frontier, and by placing moral law above the formalities of state rights, Israel was able for the first time to strike at the heart of the cancer, to arrest its growth, and to send it into headlong retreat. That is the kind of thing I mean by drastic treatment.

I believe we should study the example set by the Israelis in 1982, and debate in what circumstances, and by what means, the West as a whole will be prepared to act against terrorist states in the future. It must be made clear to the master killers of Tehran and Tripoli that there can be no ultimate hiding place for them either, that the arm of civilization is long and sinewy and may be stretched out to take them by the throat. Let us in the West consider these possibilities. Let us have no formal treaties or arrangements. But let us debate privately among ourselves when, and if so how, we will be prepared to discard the obstacle of sovereignty and national frontiers, which shelter the state terrorists. Let us calmly and discreetly amass and train the forces which will be necessary for such police action, and discuss how we will deal with the political and international consequences. Let us decide in good time the limits beyond which terrorist states will not be allowed to pass, and let us perfect a military instrument of fearful retribution when and if those limits ever are crossed.

I believe the knowledge that the civilized world has the courage and means to act in this manner will itself serve as a deterrent to state terrorism. I stress the word "courage," and the physical preparedness without which courage is useless. For the cancer of terrorism feeds on weakness in all its forms—on all the hesitations and divisions and ambiguities inseparable from free, liberal societies. We must put these weaknesses behind us, and act, in Lincoln's words, with malice toward none—except the killers; with charity for all—especially their innocent victims; above all, with firmness in the right, as God gives us to see the right. We must, as the Book of Joshua puts it, "be strong and of good courage," for it is the combination of strength and courage which alone can arrest and destroy the terrorist cancer.

II

TERRORISM AND TOTALITARIANISM

TOTALITARIANISM is the major ideological source of modern terrorism. It originated and promoted the view, so essential to today's terrorists, that there are no exemptions from politics. Politics is all, and every situation is political. Under totalitarianism the individual is always subordinate to some higher cause, whether racial, political, or religious; man is inconsequential in and of himself. Commonsense notions of truth and justice are abandoned; significantly, this abandonment is elevated to the status of a new, supposedly higher, morality. Horrendous crimes are sanctioned, not as an unavoidable evil, but as a *desirable good*, as an expression of a psychological and political liberation from a confining morality.

This, as Dostoevsky saw, is the basis of the natural affinity between the terrorist and the totalitarian. The terrorist embraces the totalitarian's substitution of immorality for morality. Like the totalitarian he believes his particular cause justifies any atrocity and endows it with moral goodness. Like him, he politicizes all of society and recognizes no restraints. This convergence of views has historically led to the alliance, and the fusion, of the terrorist and the totalitarian. Terrorism when successful has always ended in totalitarianism. Without exception, totalitarian regimes have used terrorism as a principal instrument for seizing power. Once installed, they have used it to consolidate their power and to expand it externally.

A striking example can be found in Soviet totalitarianism. The Soviet regime used terrorism to seize power and to crush internal opposition. And in recent decades the U.S.S.R. (and Soviet satellites) has encouraged various terrorist groups hostile to the West. The totalitarian states, in fact, have provided the oxygen which enables the terrorist to breathe. "The terrorist," Paul Johnson has said, "is sustained by the totalitarian tank, the torture chamber, the lash, and the secret policeman. He is the beneficiary of the Gulag Archipelago and all it stands for." That is why the rise of totalitarianism in this century, both Nazi and communist, has been inextricably linked to the rise and spread of terrorism. Both reject the true essence of politics, that is, the non-violent resolution of conflict. This shared view of human affairs is at the core of their partnership and provides the impetus for their joint assault on the West, the only political system that stands in effective opposition to them.

Terrorists, Totalitarians, and the Rule of Law

DANIEL PATRICK MOYNIHAN

THIS CENTURY has seen the development of world political culture. Institutions that were once confined to a particular state or region—the constitutional monarch, the politburo, the independent judiciary—are now available, you might say, on the world market. A world party system can be seen emerging, as the nations of the Soviet bloc, the non-aligned, and the West coalesce around particular issues and credos, and vote accordingly in international forums. Similarly, more and more nations find themselves dealing with terrorist movements whose organization and tactics are hardly distinguishable from the nineteenth-century European originals. The spread of terrorism is simply one aspect of the general diffusion of European political institutions to the world at large.

The newest addition to this European, or Western, political tradition is the totalitarian state. That has been this century's great gift to mankind.* Terrorism is a related and prior development. More or less uniformly, terrorism, when successful, ends in totalitarianism. The totalitarian state is terrorism come to power.

Such terrorism is invariably accompanied by two features. The

* The word "totalitarian" first appears in English in 1928 in a reference to fascism. In 1929 *The* (London) *Times* defined it as "a reaction against parliamentarianism . . . in favor of a 'totalitarian' or unitary state, whether Fascist or Communist."

first is the principle of a self-appointed elite (Lenin's "vanguard fighters") who decide the course of events, who shall live, who shall die. The second feature, and vastly the more dangerous, is the principle that no one is innocent of politics. Terrorism denies the distinction between state and society, public and private, government and individual, the distinction that lies at the heart of liberal belief. For the terrorist, as for the totalitarian state, there are no innocent bystanders, no private citizens. Terrorism denies that there is any private sphere, that individuals have any rights or any autonomy separate from or beyond politics.

There are thus no standards according to which the individual citizen, or the threatened society, can attempt to come to terms with the totalitarian terrorist. There is no way to satisfy his demands over time because what he wants to do is take away the capacity of others even to decide to submit. The only standard is whether one is a member of the terrorist group or not. If you are not, then there are no rules to suggest how you may be treated by this perverse elite.

The absence of standards may be put another way: *There is no law.* Law is the antithesis of both the terrorist and the totalitarian state. Law is the highest expression of liberalism, establishing as it does the distinction between the individual and society, preserving the rights of the individual vis-à-vis the state. A democratic society is ruled by law.

Terrorism seeks to destroy this law. It is unlawfulness enshrined as principle. This is why it is important that as democracies fight terrorism, as in Italy or Ireland or Israel, they do so through lawful procedures and due process, lest the terrorists win by inducing a kind of counterterrorism.

Is the United States, and generally speaking the West, sufficiently alive to the importance of asserting our adherence to the rule of law in the conduct of nations? I do not believe that we are.

We seem to be forgetting that *the law is on our side*, that the very instruments of international law were drafted to defend democracy and to oppose terrorists and totalitarians.

Shortly after leaving the United Nations, I argued in the annual survey of UN affairs of the *Harvard Journal of International Law* that if the democracies would only insist on the validity of the Charter, the United Nations was potentially a considerable asset:

> The Charter is a constitutional document utterly opposed in spirit and hostile in its provisions to totalitarianism. The Orwellian inversion of language has progressed so far in our time that it is easy to assume that no enduring meaning is to be attached to words of any sort, but this is a mistake. The meaning of the Charter is clear. It is a constitutional document drafted in the tradition of Western liberal societies.
>
> The similarities with the United States Constitution are obvious enough: "We the people of the United States . . ." "We the peoples of the United Nations . . ." The Anglo-American stress on "fundamental human rights," the "dignity and worth of the human person," and on the "equal rights of men and women" is encountered at the outset of the document and recurrently thereafter. The Charter takes as given those propositions about "human rights and . . . fundamental freedoms for all"—the common philosophical foundations on which the democratic societies of the West have been constructed. If the Soviets signed, so much the worse for them. In doing so, they undertook, as did all others, to promote, through the United Nations, "respect for human rights and for fundamental freedoms for all."

Terrorism opposes both human rights and freedom. And it is well within the rights of nations as stated in the Charter to pursue a common defense against it. The President of Sri Lanka, for example, suggested in 1984 that the United Nations consider forming a special agency devoted to stopping the spread of international terrorism. His country, of course, is merely one more example of a democratic government assaulted by a typical terrorist group, complete with the newest feature, support from distant states. The United Nations is unlikely to establish such an anti-terrorist institution. But there is no reason why members of the United Nations should not do so on their own, *as is their right under the Charter,* and in the name of its principles to help defend one another. If we are to have any success, we must be seen to be acting in support of law. That is a standard to which neutral nations can repair. We have nothing to fear from it.

The First European Terrorists

ALAIN BESANÇON

THE FIRST modern terrorism in history was initiated by the populist movement in Russia from the 1870s to the outbreak of the First World War. Much of contemporary terrorism follows the path laid by the populists at that time.

As bourgeois society in Russia became stronger, it demanded power along the lines already achieved in Western Europe, namely, representation, constitutionalism, and equal law. But a few young men of the intelligentsia were not satisfied with this program.

Possessed by an eschatological vision, they dreamed of the total salvation of mankind and of building a perfect society. They developed a doctrine which they believed scientifically proved the feasibility, indeed the inevitability, of such a historical transformation. Devoting themselves totally to this cause, they saw themselves as both heroic and rational, as they freely chose to enter into a process of general salvation that was nonetheless guided by the laws of science.

Behind this new doctrine there was a classical metaphysical, Manichean stand. This world is the theater of two forces engaged in deadly conflict—Evil and Good, Darkness and Light, Ignorance and Knowledge. Such a world deserves to be totally destroyed, opening the way to the birth of an entirely new world. Destruction is enough; the new order will emerge spontaneously. As Bakunin said, the spirit of destruction is the same as the spirit of construction. Those in possession of the doctrine must gather and organize a terrorist elite and be prepared to sacrifice their lives.

This philosophy produced two waves of terrorism. The first occurred between 1877 and 1881, the second between 1904 and 1908. Both episodes were well documented by both the police and the terrorists. The salient features are strikingly modern. Consider, for example, the second wave.

The fighting squad of the SR (Social Revolutionary) Party was an organization of about 700 young men. Supported by some 100,000 sympathizers, they were connected to the legal wing of the party only at the Central Committee level. Their methods were scientific and sophisticated. They prepared their operations with minute care and used up-to-date bombs and explosives. After their operations they usually took refuge in Finland, the first terrorist sanctuary of modern times.

Faced with such a challenge, the police had to organize a discreet anti-terrorist unit. Named the Okhrana, it numbered about 900 men, who trained and lived under pseudonyms, rarely sleeping at home. They developed a kind of mutual professional respect with the terrorists. The Okhrana's method was infiltration and recruitment of defectors through threats, promises, corruption, or more complex incentives.

But the small Okhrana, limited in its role and scope, is not to be compared with the KGB. It used neither torture nor terrorism. For example, General Gerasimov, head of the Petersburg Okhrana, was a highly intelligent, politically neutral man, who kept well within the limits of law and humanity.

For years, the tsarist government lived in the atmosphere of terror. The Tsar could not travel. The ministers were obliged to live inside the Winter Palace. Terrorist agents were found in the highest levels of the administration. Suspicion spread pervasively, poisoning social relations.

The police won, however, as they usually do. The terrorists were located, arrested, convicted, and hanged or deported. But precisely at the moment of its physical defeat, terrorism was morally victorious.

For as early as the 1870s, the terrorist organization discovered the indirect strategy: The main goal of striking against the enemy is to draw the sympathy of society. Government was the avowed target of the attacks, but the real object was civil society. With its moderate aims, its guilt-laden longings for a regular, legal, and bourgeois life, civil society feels a secret admiration for terrorist exploits and is seduced by the terrorist ethos.

Thus, during the trials of the terrorists, the public took the side of the prosecuted, helped them materially, and supported them morally. Public opinion was again laudatory when the governor of St. Petersburg was shot, and again when his murderers escaped and fled abroad. Journalists and famous writers protested whenever a terrorist was condemned to death. They expressed shock, indignation, and despair whenever the sentence was carried out. Soloviev, a great Russian philosopher, protested the hanging of the Tsar's murderers. So did Tolstoy, Leonid Andreyev, and virtually the entire literary establishment. Around the world, both progressive and conservative opinion considered the tsarist regime morally debased, disqualified, and doomed to subversive destruction.

How can this reaction be explained? It stemmed from two forces still very much alive today: political confusion and philosophical complicity. In the environment of an *"ancien régime,"* imperfect in the many ways the tsarist regime was, the normal state of affairs was one of general discontent. But we must distinguish between two extreme responses to it which, while related, are substantively different from one another—rebellion and revolution. The rebel accepts the idea of justice. He tries to restore law and justice through illegal and sometimes unjust means. But when justice is restored, in the common sense of the word, revolt ceases. In contrast, the revolutionary does not accept the common idea of justice. Justice depends upon a totally new set of social relations introduced by revolution. Justice is not the responsibility of men in positions of authority who may or may not act according to its precepts. Justice lies only in the impersonal structure of the new society, as implemented by the revolution according to doctrinal revelation. Terrorist action merely prepares the way for this social epiphany.

During the nineteenth century, the Russian cultural establishment obstinately confused revolt and revolution. The terrorist was compared with the Christian martyr or the Schillerian rebel. What is worse, the pervasive conviction survived to our time that our world is so impure, so wicked, that it does not deserve to be protected and defended.

Dostoevsky hated the Russian revolutionary, the atheistic, cosmopolitan, rootless, and ruthless "devil" (although he also abhorred the Western world and the liberal bourgeois society Russia was striving for and getting closer to). His disdain was the exception. Other great writers, if not agreeing outright with the terrorists, experienced a kind of Byronic attraction to them that remains alive today. Tolstoy, for example, was a non-violent man, but he developed a kind of sublime morality based upon rejection of personal interest, private property, and the law as such. While Tolstoy could not approve of the bomb carrier, there was nonetheless an affinity between the non-violent man of letters and the violent terrorist. Both hated the world of the bourgeois, the landlord, the policeman. Both shared the same contempt for the ordinary man, devoted to his selfish, mediocre, down-to-earth interests.

The persistence of this affinity with the terrorist among many modern intellectuals makes the assault on terrorism especially difficult, and places a special burden on those intellectuals. For if it is hard to fight terrorism on the practical plane, it is harder still to eradicate a deeply rooted nihilism in our culture that gives rise to terrorism. Terrorism grows out of a warped spiritualism, a distorted romanticism, and a deep hatred of life that drives supposedly idealistic young men to fanaticism. Curing the soul is beyond the reach and scope of the authorities. But it is not beyond the responsibility of writers, thinkers, and opinion molders.

Terrorism and the Concept of Legitimacy

LESZEK KOLAKOWSKI

DEFINING TERRORISM clearly so as to distinguish between terrorist acts and justified political violence is often difficult today. Partly this results from the general degradation of our political language—the lines between "liberation" and "tyranny" have likewise been obscured. In the nineteenth century it was clear what terrorism was: assassination campaigns directed at government officials by opposition groups (such as anarchists and populists in Russia) who aimed to undermine the established power. Indeed, these terrorists applied the term to themselves. Nowadays, of course, no one admits to being a terrorist, just as no one admits to opposing freedom, peace, and democracy.

Our uncertainty about when to apply the word "terrorist" is the reverse side of our confusion about the concept of legitimacy. Democratic states are compelled by the international situation to recognize the legitimacy of many despotic regimes—some of which sponsor terrorism—and have thus themselves helped to obscure the distinction between recognizing a *government* (which implies merely that it is effectively in control of a country) and recognizing the *legitimacy* of that government (which implies a popular mandate). Many states that have emerged since the Second World War, especially those in the Third World, have never known anything resembling democratic politics; in some, politicians have traditionally competed with one another by assassinating their rivals.

Communism provides an easy path to ideological legitimacy for many of these regimes, whether they are communist or not. As understood in communist doctrine, legitimacy does not derive from any mechanism whereby society confers power on any group or individual, but is purely the result of an ideological assertion: those in power simply declare that they embody the interests and aspirations of the people, of the nation, of all mankind, regardless of whether they can offer any proof to support these claims. The very existence of the United Nations, which includes among its members some clearly gangster states, is not helpful in this respect, for it confers on all members the same international legitimacy. And there exists no effective mechanism whereby states that practice international terrorism can be branded as international outlaws.

Since the distinction between these two kinds of recognition has become unclear, when a state employs terror its legitimacy is not weakened in the opinion of other states. The distinction becomes blurred as well between the sometimes violent struggle against oppression and despotism, on the one hand, and terrorism aimed at the destruction of democratic institutions, on the other. Thus, the armed struggle of the underground partisans against the Nazi occupation, for example, was perfectly legitimate, because the rule of the invaders had no legitimacy whatsoever. In contrast, terrorism against democracies such as Italy or West Germany is clearly illegitimate.

Modern totalitarianism has also helped muddle the question of legitimacy. Rather than establish a particularly cruel and repressive law, totalitarian states effectively abolish law altogether. What is characteristic of totalitarianism is a form of law consisting of lawlessness—that is, the law's independence as a mediator between society and the state is destroyed. Legal codes, especially those that apply to political matters, are deliberately vague, designed to give a free hand to the executive power (which is identical to the legislative and judicial powers) in jailing or killing anyone it wishes. Thus the worst atrocities committed by the Soviet government against its own people, including the genocide during Stalin's regime, have been for the most part entirely "legal." Although state terror has been considerably restricted since Stalin's time, the principle that the law cannot restrict the prerogatives of the executive has never been abrogated. Since the legitimacy of the overwhelming power of the state rests entirely on ideology ("We rule because we express the historical interests of the society, of the working class, of the nation," etc.), the insistence on the primacy of this ideology is absolutely essential, whether anyone takes it seriously or not. The ruling power is *always* right in its struggles against all enemies, internal or external, real or imagined. Therefore, terrorism against other states—whether it involves assassinating troublesome defectors or even foreign leaders such as the Pope—is always justified.

Communist countries, with some obvious exceptions (Russia and Poland during the early years of communist rule, Hungary during the revolution), have never experienced terrorism directed against the state. The only organized democratic resistance that has ever existed in a communist country, Solidarity in Poland in 1980–81, never employed violence against the state, although it had the practical means to do so. All the political violence in Poland was employed by the government. In part, the efficiency and size of the secret police in communist countries accounts for the relative absence of terrorism there. The openness of democratic societies, by contrast, not only allows terrorists easy access to arms and false documents and gives them relative freedom of movement; it makes their job less dangerous—if they are caught, they are rarely tortured or executed. But there is an ideological reason as well for the proliferation of Soviet-backed terrorism in the West: the very existence of democracy is intolerable to totalitarian regimes. It is not the supposed military threat or the widely cited feeling of "insecurity" which compels the Soviet Union to try to destroy democratic institutions all over the world. It is the simple fact that the ideological legitimacy of the communist power system must always appear grotesque so long as democratic countries exist.

But there remain painful problems in defining legitimacy today; criteria that would be universally applicable are difficult to find. In many countries, it is impossible to determine the degree of popular support enjoyed by the government. And in any case, some cruel or despotic systems may be popular, at least for a time, and can therefore make claims to legitimacy. This was certainly true for some years in Nazi Germany; Iran's barbarous theocracy might have made similar claims. But the concept is clear enough when political violence is directed against countries where legal forms exist for political opposition to operate openly, for political conflict to be resolved peacefully, and where the rights of minorities are respected. Terror directed against the legitimate authorities in such a state amounts to the waging of *civil* war and should be treated as such. Terror directed against one state by another is simply war and should be treated accordingly.

Terrorism, Marxism, and the Soviet Constitution

WOLFGANG FIKENTSCHER

To UNDERSTAND HOW the Soviet Union justifies terrorist strategies in its foreign policy we must look at the basics of Marxism and the new Soviet Constitution of 1977, especially the Preamble and the important Articles 28 to 31. The theoretical center of Marxism is the Labor Value Theory. Developed by Marx and still accepted by all branches of Marxism, this theory stipulates that the value of each amount of labor or merchandise can be determined by either the exchange value or the use value.

The *exchange value* is formed in the marketplace. As the instrument by which labor is "exploited," the exchange value is responsible for a host of evils: the formation of the class system, social alienation, division of labor, capital accumulation, political crises, imperialism. But in the absence of exploitation, the true value of goods produced by labor is the *use value* of labor. It denotes the values of life in terms of necessity, not utility. The use value cannot be measured in the marketplace; it cannot be tested, debated, argued about. It is an ideal entity which can only be determined "scientifically," in a method that is not, however, open to debate and argumentation. Though use values are considered by subordinate planning authorities, in the final analysis they are determined by the Politburo, whose powers are "scientifically" fixed beyond dispute. Socialism is what the

[52]

Kremlin says it is. *Pravda*, the truth, is made by the "competent," and competence is a function of power.

Armed with its mandate as the ultimate repository of socialist truth, the Politburo can apply its definition of socialism worldwide. Indeed, Article 28 of the U.S.S.R. Constitution empowers it to do so. According to this article, the foreign policy of the Soviet Union is "directed toward the strengthening of the positions of World Socialism, the assistance of the peoples in their fight for national liberation and social progress . . ." This assistance includes, under Article 31, the use of the Soviet Army and Navy for the "defense of socialist achievements," the definitions of which are again to be determined by the Politburo.

Such defense can also include state-directed or -supported terrorism, an instrument that is far cheaper and less risky than direct military means. The theoretical Marxist acceptance of terror as an instrument of the class struggle has always been ambiguous, as can already be seen with Marx himself, and with Lenin and some of his followers. In practice, the attitude of Marxism to terror is often a matter of hindsight. Terror which advances the aims of the Marxist cadres is considered a successful and necessary revolutionary action. Terror which produces negative results is branded "individual," "bourgeois," "isolated," or "counterrevolutionary," and is therefore *a posteriori* rejected. In the end, this judgment is made by the leading cadres on grounds of "scientific" values. Right and wrong are determined within the party, and made politically binding *ex cathedra* by the same doctrinal authority that is empowered to fix all truths, including the use value theory.

A Marxist government does not act all that differently from any Marxist party, movement, or self-appointed avant-garde. But a government needs a more formal legal rationale for its conduct. For the Soviets this is found in Articles 28–31 of the Soviet Constitution, which reformulate Lenin's idea of a "peace policy" into a legal text. According to this doctrine, a worldwide class struggle is being waged among the socialist, capitalist, and developing worlds. The balance of power, however, is steadily shifting to the "socialist world system." Soviet foreign policy plays an important role in this struggle. It incorporates when necessary the "principle of peaceful coexistence," which favors the fight of the working class in capitalist countries and the "freedom fight" of the colonial and dependent peoples. This principle by no means renounces a violent solution to the conflict between the systems. Indeed, it has been correctly said that Soviet assistance to "national liberation wars" instigates violence within the Third World, harms the development of peaceful relations between socialist and capitalist states, and increases the chances of conflict. Peaceful coexistence, Soviet-style, does not mean recognizing the legitimacy of the adversary. It merely accepts the *fact* of his existence as a given condition for a limited time.

The defeat of the Red Army in its "revolutionary war" against Poland in 1920 forced Lenin to reformulate Soviet foreign-policy goals. He allowed for a temporary coexistence of the Soviet Union in the international framework of capitalist states, even at the price of a postponed world revolution. In 1977, the specter of nuclear war induced the Soviet rulers to adopt again this "peace policy" as a "continued strategic guideline" of Soviet foreign policy. By then it was impossible to deny that the nuclear stalemate was a serious obstacle to Lenin's eschatological theory of revolution and war. Since the revolutionary People's War is a good war, waging war is not bad as such; waging nuclear war therefore cannot in itself be ruled out for the Soviet Union. But the unprecedented dangers of a nuclear war and the resulting stalemate affect the prospects of victory in that part of Lenin's "peace policy" devoted to the revolutionary conquest of the world.

How then to adjust this "peace policy," basically a war strategy against the rest of the world, to the conditions of the nuclear age? The solution is to reduce the risks of waging war below the level of nuclear risk. One way of doing this is *hidden* warfare, including terrorist activities. The necessity of staying below the nuclear threshold and the self-imposed duty to militarily guard the "socialist achievements" are both implicitly addressed in Article 28 of the Soviet Constitution. The Soviet Union is permitted to foment virtually all kinds of unrest, and to physically intervene with its own forces or with surrogates when a critical point is reached. Destabilization is enshrined as a constitutional principle.

Totalitarian regimes thus tend to be totalitarian not only toward their own subjects but also toward the outside world. They reject law, domestic or international, whenever it does not coincide with their totalitarian mission. Significantly, the Leninist "peace policy" embodied in the Soviet Constitution prescribes assistance to "peoples" in their fight for "social progress." Yet while the Soviet Constitution uses the term "peoples," international law, with its commitment to keep peace under Article II of the United Nations Charter, addresses "states." The communist conception invites active interference and subversion in the affairs of other states. Whenever the fight of a "people" for "Progress" may result in "socialist achievements"—all three notions to be determined by the Politburo—the Soviet Constitution, guided by Leninist revolutionary theory, justifies either open warfare (Article 31) or hidden warfare (Article 28). And the latter obviously includes the practice or support of terrorism.

The Totalitarian Confusion

JEANE J. KIRKPATRICK

THE FIRST STEP in understanding politics is to see things as they are, without confusion or mystification—simply to observe who does what to whom. What the terrorist does is kill, maim, kidnap, torture. His victims may be schoolchildren, travelers, industrialists, political leaders, diplomats. Terrorists' victims may have no particular political identification, like the diners in a Paris restaurant or the travelers passing through Lod airport in Israel, or they may be powerful political symbols, like Aldo Moro or Pope John Paul II.

The terrorist chooses violence as the instrument of first resort. Yet terrorism differs from simple crime, which can also be defined as unauthorized violence against people who are not at war. The difference lies not in the act itself but in the terrorist's understanding, however vague, of what he is doing. The terrorist's motive is political in a way that the criminal's is not. The terrorist acts in the name of some public purpose. The members of Lucky Luciano's Murder Inc. acted for private purposes. John Hinckley, as I understand it, attempted to kill President Reagan for essentially private reasons. The terrorists who sprayed bullets into a Paris restaurant, like those who attempted to murder the Pope, had a political goal. Terrorism is a form of political war.

Terrorism should also be distinguished from conventional war, and terrorists from soldiers. One of the main differences is this: A soldier uses violence where a state of belligerence is recognized to exist, and against armed enemies; a terrorist engages in violence against people who do not understand themselves to be at war and, in fact, are not at war. The victims of terrorist attacks are unarmed, undefended, and unwary. The crucial point is that they conceive of themselves as civilians. They do not understand that they are regarded by the terrorist as belligerents in an ongoing war. Terrorist war is part of a total war, which sees the whole of society as the enemy and all the members of society as appropriate objects for violence. It is absolute war because its goal is the absolute destruction of a society. Terrorists are the shock troops in a war to the death against the values and institutions of a society and of the people who embody it.

The affinities between terrorism and totalitarianism are multiple. Both politicize society. The totalitarian makes society, culture, and even personality the objects of his plans and actions; the terrorist sees the whole of society as the object of his violence and his war. Both regard violence as an appropriate means to their political ends. Both use it as the instruments of first resort. Both reject the basic moral principles of Judeo-Christian civilization. Both act in the name of a higher morality, whose transcendent ends demand the violation of conventional morality and the sacrifice of people whose membership in the old society makes them expendable. Both encourage the expression of murderous instincts, whose repression, Freud correctly emphasized, is a precondition of civilization. The relations of both totalitarians and terrorists to others are dominated by hostile intent: the enemy is everywhere, struggle is inevitable, war is total.

But there are two other important links between totalitarianism and terrorism. First, the most powerful totalitarian state of our time is also the principal supporter and sponsor of international terrorism. Second, those who pursue power by using terrorism generally aspire to form totalitarian societies. As Orwell wrote, "It is not merely that power corrupts, so also do the ways of attaining power. Therefore, all efforts to regenerate society by violent means lead to the cellars of the NKVD. The essential act is the rejection of democracy—that is, of the underlying values of democracy. Once you have decided upon that, Stalin, or at any rate someone like Stalin, is already under way."

The choice of method is the essential political act. It is hardly surprising, then, that rulers who choose coercion as an instrument of government should see violence as the preeminent means of extending their political dominion. In the late 1960s, Soviet theorists began to emphasize the "armed road" as the way to achieve power in the Western Hemisphere. They have set about supporting terrorist groups in this hemisphere. The Bandera Roja in Venezuela, the FMLN in El Salvador, the FSLN in Nicaragua, and the Montaneros in Argentina are just a few of the small bands of violent men who have been supported in their efforts by Soviet-bloc countries. These technicians in violence and propaganda are called national liberation movements.

Such groups use terror to inspire fear and produce a revolutionary situation; this has become the preferred tactic in contemporary revolutionary conflict. The Russians frankly acknowledge that their support for such movements may be crucial. For example, they say: "National liberation struggle is a form of war waged by people of colonial and dependent, or formerly colonial, territories, in which socialist countries become the decisive factor when people launch an armed struggle against internal reactionaries." The United Nations' acceptance of so-called national liberation movements as legitimate is as good an indicator as any of the moral confusion that has come to surround this view of violence as the preferred method of political action.

Since the 1970s, the UN General Assembly has passed numerous resolutions asserting its support for the right of the PLO and other "national liberation movements" to "struggle by all means . . . to achieve power." The General Assembly majority has proclaimed that these movements have the right to employ violence, in fact saying that terrorist violence in defense of national liberation is no crime. It has so consistently condemned countries for attempting to defend themselves against terrorist violence that an operational principle seems to have been established. The distinction between legitimate and illegitimate use of force has not so much been blurred as stood on its head. Where recognized states were once seen as having a monopoly on the legitimate use of violence, "liberation movements" are now seen as having such a monopoly.

The intellectual and moral confusion is deep. Unable to distinguish between force used to liberate and force used to enslave, a majority of nations in the UN regard legitimacy as a function of the will and power exercised on behalf of "national liberation movements." Yet we know better. We know that it cannot be that terror wreaked on a civilian population by a revolutionary movement is liberation, while force used by a government responding to that threat is repression.

There is one last affinity between totalitarianism and terrorism. Both attempt to confuse as well as to terrorize. Orwell, Solzhenitsyn, and others have said that in totalitarian societies violence is used to maintain a system of lies, and lies are used to justify relations based on violence. Violence can be used to close a society. Lies can be used to veil the violence—to call open that which is closed, true that which is false, insane he who raises questions. Finding the courage to face the truth and speak about it is surely the first step toward the defeat of those who would destroy our freedom and our world.

III

TERRORISM AND THE ISLAMIC WORLD

TOTALITARIANISM is not the only wellspring of modern terrorism. Other ideological, national, and religious movements have spawned terrorist groups. But in recent years, few terrorists have matched the international prominence of those backed by the more extreme proponents of Islamic fundamentalism and, equally, Arab nationalism.

Certain strains of Islam promote an uncompromising interpretation of the faith which divides the world into Muslim and infidel, and enjoins the former to wage unremitting warfare against the latter. To be sure, the choice of infidels is vast, not least among the practitioners of Islam itself who do not meet the stringent test of doctrinal purity. Indeed, a considerable number of Islamic terrorism's victims have been Muslim. Yet its main energies have been directed toward the outside. In the non-Muslim world, the main focus of this hatred has been the Western world. The West has been traditionally viewed by Muslims as responsible for the historical containment, humiliation, and defeat of Islam. The resurgence of Islamic fundamentalism in recent decades has given that ancient animus new life and, through terrorism, new expression. To this should be added the rise of Pan-Arabism, paralleling and often overlapping the resurgence of Islam, which views the West in essentially the same terms.

Terrorism is thus uniquely pervasive in the Middle East, the

[61]

part of the world in which Islam is dominant. And it is dispro-
portionately from this region that much of the terrorism in other
parts of the world emanates. It is, in fact, impossible to conceive
of international terrorism without the Middle East as both locus
and source of so much terrorist activity. This was not always the
case in this century. Political violence, particularly the long tradition of assassinating adversaries, was given new life when independent Arab regimes emerged after World War II. Islamic
fundamentalism's antagonism to modern political institutions,
and the volatile nature of Arab political institutions, gave rise to
continual bloodshed and instability. Middle Eastern states arose
which, with few exceptions, recognized neither the national
boundaries nor the political legitimacy of their neighbors. The
use of terrorism became not an incidental activity of governments
but often a pillar of state policy, the principal instrument against
domestic and foreign enemies. This is why the term "terrorist
states" has been fittingly applied to so many regimes in the
Middle East.

The Qaddafi regime in Libya, for example, is less a government and more a murderous clique. But like other such regimes,
it has taken full advantage of the immunities and privileges that
the international order confers on legally constituted states, all
the while ignoring the most basic rules of international conduct.
The addition of Iran to the roster of terrorist states was a wa-
tershed development in the spread of terrorism from the Middle
East, for Iran is the first full-fledged, overtly *Islamic*, terrorist
state. And the effects of this change are being widely felt, from
the attacks against American targets by Islamic terrorists to the
increased agitation in several countries of Southeast Asia by
Islamic minorities and populations.

The antagonism of Islamic and Arab radicalism to the West is
frequently misunderstood. It is sometimes explained as deriving
from American support for Israel. But the hostility to the West
preceded the creation of Israel by centuries, and much of the
terrorists' animus is directed against targets and issues that have
nothing to do with Israel. Indeed, the relationship is most often
the other way around. Middle Eastern radicals did not develop
their hatred for the West because of Israel; they hated Israel

from its inception *because it is an organic part of the West.* That is, because Israel represents for them precisely the incarnation of those very traditions and values, foremost of which is democracy, which they hate and fear.

This deep anti-West sentiment has fostered a seemingly bizarre collaboration between Arab and Islamic radicalism and communist totalitarianism. Though Islamic radicalism is opposed to communist secularism, their common antagonism to the West has often united them. Worlds apart in other matters, they join in utterly rejecting the central democratic tenet, that the governing authority is derived from popular consent and not from a religious or ideological decree. Both Islamic fundamentalists and communist totalitarians view the expansion, even the existence, of democratic ideas as inherently threatening to their own authority. This is how it is possible, indeed common, to find radical groups professing to be at the same time both Islamic and Marxist. The West will not be able to stem the tide of international terrorism without first facing squarely this alliance in terror.

Islamic Terrorism?

BERNARD LEWIS

WHY DO WE SPEAK of Islamic terrorists? When we speak of the
Tupamaros, Montaneros, and other exotically named groups in
Latin America, we do not speak of them as Catholic terrorists
or talk of terrorism in Catholic countries, nor do we use similar
denominational descriptions for terrorist groups in Europe.

Why Islam? Is it because, as has at times been stated of late,
Islam as a religion is particularly conducive to terrorism or even
tolerant of terrorism?

I think one may affirm without hesitation that this is not so.
Islam, after all, is one of the great religions of the world and
shares with its sister religions a commitment to moral values,
moral standards, and moral laws, and condemns the maltreat-
ment of the innocent. Islamic law, for example, states quite
explicitly that no man shall suffer for the offense of another. At
a very early date, in discussing the conduct of warfare, it laid
down rules which were humane concerning the treatment of
non-combatants. Generally speaking, Muslims, like Christians,
Jews, and followers of other religions, are against and not for
terrorism, and share the sense of shock that terrorism evokes.
Terrorism of the modern kind, directed against bystanders, non-
combatants, and the innocent is not Islamic. It is as much an
importation to the Islamic world as are the bombs and guns
which terrorists use.

Nevertheless, it is appropriate to use Islam as a term of def-

[65]

inition and classification in discussing present-day terrorism for two reasons.

The first is the essentially political character which the Islamic religion has had from its very foundation and retains to the present day. An intimate association between religion and politics, between power and cult, marks a principal distinction between Islam and other religions. Islam is a political religion. This can be seen if we compare even the sacred scriptural histories which mark the beginnings of Islam with those of other religions.

The founder of Christianity died on the cross. Moses died before being permitted to enter the Promised Land. Muhammad the Prophet of Islam, in contrast, founded a state and governed it. As the Ayatollah Khomeini has recently reminded us, Muhammad was a sovereign. He promulgated laws. He dispensed justice. He collected taxes. He levied armies. He made war, he made peace. He did all the things a head of state does. And, therefore, politics, government, law, war and peace are all part of the Holy Law of Islam.

The second reason is the reassertion of this association of Islam and politics at the present time. In the course of the centuries, the ways of the Islamic world were much modified, particularly in the last hundred years. In some regions modernization, Westernization, and secularization brought about certain changes and a measure of separation—I won't say between church and state, since this would be a meaningless formulation in relation to Islam, but at least between political and religious matters.

The resurgence of Islam, fashionably called fundamentalist, has as one of its main grievances precisely the removal of this religious quality of political and public life, and expresses the desire to return to an Islamic society governed by Islamic law and ruled by an Islamic state.

Given this inherently religious character of politics and the inherently political character of religion, given that Islam is the basis of authority, identity, loyalty, legitimacy in power, even of an ideology of revolt against power, it is Islam that provides the most powerful critique of the old order and the most acceptable formulation of aspirations for a new. Islam has proved itself, again and again, to be the most effective and perhaps the only really effective system of ideas, symbols, and slogans for the mobilization of the Muslim masses.

Thus it is inevitable that when the Islamic world confronts the problem of terrorism, that problem, too, assumes a religious, indeed in a sense an Islamic, aspect. In traditional Islam and therefore also in resurgent fundamentalist Islam, God is the sole source of sovereignty. God is the head of the state. The state is God's state. The army is God's army. The treasury is God's treasury, and the enemy, of course, is God's enemy.

This formulation has fearsome consequences, which will be immediately obvious. Violent conflict as perceived in Islamic law and tradition, and as expressed in Islamic history, is of two main types: the conflict against the external enemy and the conflict against the internal enemy. And it is in connection with the second that the issue of terrorism has most frequently arisen, both in the more distant past and at the present time.

The first conflict, that between the world of Islam and the outside world of unbelievers, is a struggle which according to law may be halted by truces, but can be ended only by the final conversion or subjugation of the unbelievers. In Islamic doctrine, this war is to be conducted with due warning and declarations to the enemy on the eve of hostilities, and with the observance of the laws of war—not the ones we know at the present time, but the ones laid down in Islamic law. And these leave no place for what might be called terrorism, even by the wider definitions that have been proffered.

The other and much more relevant form of armed conflict or the use of violence is internal, where violence is called upon to defend God's state or, alternatively, to remove those who have somehow violated and usurped it. The *locus classicus* occurred in A.D. 656, with the killing of the third caliph of Islam, the Caliph Uthman.

A debate then began which has continued to the present day. There were some who said that the Caliph was murdered, and that those who killed him were murderers subject to the penalties of the law. There were others who said that the Caliph was a tyrant and a usurper, that he was violating God's law, that his blood therefore was forfeit, and that those who killed him were not murderers but the executors of God's will. The second group came to be known as the Shiites, and the argument has continued ever since.

The life of the Prophet Muhammad is the model for Muslim conduct in all matters. We must remember, however, that there are two phases in his career. I have already referred to one phase, when he was the head of a state which he had formed in Medina. But earlier he also had been a rebel against the existing oligarchy in Mecca. Thus, there are two prophetic models: the prophet as rebel and the prophet as ruler. In the writings on this there are two continuing traditions which can be seen in Islamic law, thought, and history: the quietist tradition, calling for submission to authority, and the activist tradition, often associated with, though by no means completely identified with, Shiism.

Shiism produced a number of radical, activist groups, one of which came to be known during the Middle Ages as the Assassins. They took out the patent on the term, though hardly on the practice. The Assassins are perhaps the archetypal example of the organized use of violence and murder directed against carefully selected individuals. They offer the first real example in history of systematically planned terrorism conducted over a long period of time, directed against carefully chosen and designated enemies for the accomplishment of certain purposes.

Assassin terrorism differs somewhat from the modern kind. The Assassins assassinated only rulers, ministers, and generals. And while I suppose that from the point of view of rulers, ministers, and generals this is deplorable, it does not qualify for comparison with the kind of terrorism prevalent today.

Another significant difference is that the Assassins never used missiles, poisons, or other indirect weapons. They were always direct. The Assassin went right up to his victim and normally made no attempt whatsoever to escape. There are some modern parallels—for example, in the murder of Sadat. The purpose was, of course, to terrify; and in this they achieved success. Rulers, generals, and ministers often modified their conduct because of the danger of assassination. In an autocratic regime, the removal of the autocrat, or even the threat to remove him, could bring significant change.

A medieval Persian historian tells us the story of a certain theologian, one Fakhr al-Din Razi, who used to write polemics attacking the Assassins. One evening he was sitting at his desk and writing. Suddenly from nowhere a man appeared before him and said, "My master has sent me to ask, Why do you attack us." The theologian said, "Of course, because you are in error." The man produced a knife, dug it into the desk, and said, "This could easily have been you." The theologian admitted this was so. Said the emissary of the Assassin chief, "If you continue to write against us, the next time it *will* be you. However, if you change your views"—here he produced a bag of gold from under his cloak—"then this will be offered to you." At this point, says the chronicler, the theologian in question modified his views and began to write more favorably about the Assassins. When he was asked by a colleague why he had changed his attitude, he answered, "They have arguments that are both weighty and penetrating."

The terrorism of the medieval Assassins lasted several centuries. It expressed the smoldering discontent and the continuing resentments of a society in which rapid changes were taking place. It made a tremendous impact. It terrorized a series of regimes. But it ended in total failure. The Assassins disappeared, having accomplished none of their purposes.

Political Terrorism in the Muslim World

ELIE KEDOURIE

THERE IS A prevalent—and justifiable—impression that an ap-
preciable part of terrorist activities today originate, and frequently take place, in the world of Islam, and particularly in its
Arab portion. The Western public has become acutely aware of
these activities owing to the electronic media, and their ability
to speedily report terrorist outrages in a graphic and striking
manner. But the fact that political terrorism originating in the
Muslim and Arab world is constantly in the headlines must not
obscure the perhaps more significant fact that this terrorism has
an old history. More significant, because this old history will
serve to account for, and in great measure explain, the recourse
to political terrorism today, which will thus be seen to be more
than simply a passing contemporary phenomenon—to be, on the
contrary, a phenomenon by no means easy to eradicate.

The first political assassination to take place in Islam is that
of Ali, the cousin and son-in-law of the Prophet, who became
the fourth Caliph. He was murdered in the year 661 of the Christian era by a member of a group of his former followers who
came to believe that Ali had adopted a policy at variance with
the word of God. Much better known, of course, much more
formidable and longer lasting, were the Assassins, an offshoot of
the Ismaili Shiites who established the Fatimid Caliphate in
Cairo in 969. The Assassins were votaries of a religion which

held that the only legitimate ruler of the Muslims was the descendant of Ismail, himself seventh in the line of succession from Ali, in their eyes the sole legitimate legatee of the Prophet. Under the impulsion of a leader of genius, Hasan-i Sabbah (d. 1124), who, as Bernard Lewis has shown (*The Assassins*, 1967), may be considered as a foremost exponent of the theory and practice of terrorism, comparatively small groups of Ismailis in eastern Persia and Syria perfected assassination as a weapon against Sunni rulers and their officials, as well as against Crusader leaders. The Assassins held that terrorism was an efficient weapon because, as an Ismaili writer put it, "by one single warrior on foot a king may be stricken with terror, though he own more than a hundred thousand horsemen." Such a belief held a certain plausibility for Assassins because of the character of the states against which they pitted themselves. These were centralized despotisms in which, to adopt Hegel's description of Oriental realms, one man alone was free. To do away with this man and, possibly, with his immediate entourage seemed to offer an easy way of toppling a regime. Centralized despotism has, by and large, continued to characterize the world of Islam, where the gap between ruler and ruled has, if anything, increased in modern times, and where one finds a noticeable lack of political institutions which articulate the body politic and give it strength and resilience. But, in the end, the Assassins failed. However many rulers and their servants they managed to murder, they could not possibly prevail against the organized military power, resting on an extensive territorial base, of the rulers they challenged. In this respect, what is true of the Assassins would generally hold true of terrorism in the modern world, including the world of Islam.

The Assassins sent out by Hasan-i Sabbah and his lieutenants were known as *fidais* or *fidawis*, i.e., those who offer themselves up in sacrifice for the sake of their cause. The expression, as well as the phenomenon, has survived. It has come to be used by terrorists who emerged in another Shiite society—that of the Twelver Shiites, i.e., those Shiites who believe that the legitimate ruler of the Muslims is the twelfth descendant of Ali, who disappeared in about 873. This imam, now hidden, will reappear in his own good time, and will be recognized as the Mahdi, the rightly guided one, the Master of the Hour, Living Proof and Bringer of Resurrection. In Twelver Shiism, therefore, there is a built-in Messianism. This Messianism has usually encouraged political passivity, but it can also fuel political activism of an extreme kind, and lead to terrorist acts, as with the Assassins. The activities from the mid-forties to the mid-fifties of this century, in Iran, of the Fedayan-i Islam, led by a cleric who called himself Nawab Safevi, are a case in point. They assassinated the prime minister, Razmara, and a well-known writer, Kasravi, who held anti-Islamic views. The same Messianic radicalism and readiness for self-sacrifice marks those Iranian devotees of Ayatollah Khomeini thought to have been responsible for the suicidal attacks in 1983 on the U.S. Embassy in Beirut and on United States, French, and Israeli bases in Beirut and Tyre, as well as those who, during the same year, attacked the U.S. Embassy and other public buildings in Kuwait.

The Ismailis organized their activities from the safety of fortified castles dominating a comparatively exiguous hinterland. After the establishment of the Islamic republic in Iran, terrorism came to enjoy a sanctuary considerably less vulnerable and facilities much more extensive than Hasan-i Sabbah could have dreamed of. Khomeini's Iran thus exemplifies the idea of a "terrorist state"—a state which, as a matter of course, organizes terrorist activities against foreign individuals and groups whom it desires to eliminate or intimidate. Of this now useful, albeit ghastly, concept, the evidence shows that the U.S.S.R., Syria, Libya, and Iraq offer further exemplifications.

Terrorism in the world of Islam has other roots, which come from Europe. Modern European political thought and attitudes have a prominent strand of messianic activism and violence— of what can be called ideological thuggery. This feature of European political thought and attitudes became part of the worldwide market of ideas and eventually passed, with much else, into the world of Islam. One of the earliest figures associated with terrorism, in theory and practice, was the well-known Jamal al-Din al-Afghani (1838–97), whose activities ranged over a large part of the Muslim world. Afghani was a Shiite, and his thought is a strange amalgam of Western and Eastern notions. He certainly believed in assassination. While in Egypt, in the late 1870s, together with his disciple Muhammad Abduh (later Mufti of Egypt), he plotted the assassination of the Khedive Ismail. This plot came to nothing, but some two decades later, while at Constantinople, Afghani successfully encompassed the murder of Nasir al-Din Shah. The simple-minded murderer whom he dispatched to Tehran, when caught and interrogated, gave expression to ideas partly European, partly Shiite, which unmistakably carried the stamp of Afghani's inspiration. He referred to the bloodshed which accompanied the French Revolution as his justification, and avowed the belief that Afghani was the Mahdi, who will rid the earth of injustice and fill it with justice.

A more purely European provenance is usual in terrorist movements and activities in the world of Islam during this century. This is the case with Wardany, a French-educated Muslim pharmacist who murdered the Coptic prime minister of Egypt, Butros Ghali, in 1910, and who, awaiting execution in his prison cell, was busy reading Bagehot's *British Constitution* and Rousseau's *Social Contract*, and sketching a political treatise to deal with the constitution of a future Islamic government. In the second and third decades of this century, Egypt also saw a proliferation of secret terrorist groups connected with nationalist parties, and particularly with the Wafd, who believed that the murder of British officials would do away with British dominance and inaugurate a new heaven and a new earth. Nasser, as he tells us in *The Philosophy of the Revolution*, was himself attracted as a young man by the lure, the excitement, and the romanticism of terrorist murder. So was his successor as President of Egypt, Anwar al-Sadat, who, at the end of the Second World War, was implicated in a political assassination. In Algeria, again, in the 1940s and the early '50s, Messali al-Hadj's overt political party had a secret Special Organization attached to it, the function of which was to engage in terrorism. Messali began his career as a communist organizer among Algerian workers in France. Many members of his Special Organization were later to form the leadership of the FLN—itself very much, in many ways, a terrorist organization.

The Palestine Liberation Organization is the best-known body in the Muslim world to derive its doctrine and practice from a European model. The PLO came into prominence after the Six-Day War, when the West Bank and the Gaza Strip were conquered by Israel. Its doctrine then was that its guerrillas would challenge the Israeli army in the conquered territories, these guerrillas being sheltered by, and finding cover among, sympathizing local populations. The PLO would thus be applying the tactics of Chinese and Vietnamese communists. They would circulate in the occupied territories like "fish in water." This strategy speedily failed, and *guerilla* action was replaced by terrorist activity properly speaking against Israeli, Arab, and foreign civilian targets. This has remained the dominant strategy of the PLO, any attempt to transform it into a regular military force or people's militia having so far failed, like the terrorist strategy itself.

We have to consider another group of terrorists, extremely active over the last few years, whose inspiration is different. These are connected with, or stem from, the movement of the Muslim Brethren, which Hasan al-Banna formed in Egypt in the late 1920s. The movement originally aimed at the regeneration of Islam in Egyptian society—a society corrupted and pulverized through European domination and godless European ideas.

To pursue such an ideal was necessarily to be involved in politics, and Banna's movement came increasingly to aspire to a political role. By the outbreak of the Second World War, the Brethren had become a political force and Banna an important political personage able to mobilize large numbers of followers. In order to realize his goals, Banna created and controlled a secret Special Apparatus which was used for clandestine activities, including assassinations. These activities must have alarmed the authorities considerably, and Banna himself was assassinated in 1949, reportedly on the orders of King Faruk.

The military regime which replaced the monarchy in 1952 seemed at first well-disposed to the Brethren, the "Free Officers," including Nasser and Sadat, having had secret dealings with Banna and his lieutenants and having shown sympathy for their aims. But the military regime and the Brethren were soon in conflict. When, in 1954, an attempt was made to assassinate Nasser, the Brethren were held responsible. They were suppressed and driven underground, and many of their leaders executed or imprisoned. Among these was one of the ablest of the Brethren, Sayyid Qutb, who was to remain in prison, apart from a short interval, between 1954 and 1966, when he was in turn condemned to death and executed. What brought about such harsh treatment was the publication in 1965 of a short book of his, *Signposts on the Road*, which the military regime considered so subversive and dangerous that it was moved to publish a rejoinder, *Signposts on the Road to Treason and Reaction.*

Qutb taught that sovereignty belonged only to God, and that existing rulers, by disregarding this divine truth, and by claiming to exercise a merely terrestrial sovereignty, proved themselves to be unbelievers and usurping tyrants. With such rulers the Muslims could in no way compromise, and to them no obedience was due. This doctrine seems to be the inspiration of a number of terrorist activities in Egypt, all based on the premise that the actual ruler of Egypt possessed no legitimacy and that it was mandatory to kill him. The year 1974 saw a conspiracy to kill Sadat organized by a Palestinian, Salih Sirriya, who was caught and executed. In 1977, another terrorist outrage was perpetrated against a man of religion who was Minister of Pious Foundations. This was organized by an Egyptian, Shukri Mustafa, a former member of the Brethren, who formed a group of Muslims popularly known as the Group of Excommunication and Withdrawal; Shukri preached the withdrawal of the faithful, i.e., his followers, from the general Islamic society, which he anathematized as one of unbelief, *kufr*—hence the appellation of his group. Following the murder, Shukri was caught and executed. Lastly, there was the Jihad, or Holy War Group, from which Sadat's assassin was to emerge, who were inspired by an electrician, Abd al-Salam Faraj, author of an opuscule, *The Hidden Duty*. The duty in question, which, for the author, was hidden, and as much a pillar of Islam as other, publicly acknowledged, obligations, was that of killing the Muslim ruler who compromises with unbelievers and unbelief. Sadat was one such ruler. This conviction led the twenty-four-year-old Lieutenant Khalid al-Islambuli to organize Sadat's murder. Having done the deed, Islambuli declared that he had just killed Pharaoh.

The Muslim Brethren in Syria have likewise engaged in terrorist activities. Their target is the Baathist regime, which, in their eyes, is doubly reprehensible. Baathist doctrine is secularist, and for nearly two decades now the Baathist regime has been controlled by a faction of Alawites—in Sunni eyes, heretics beyond the pale. The Brethren organized the murder of numerous Baathist officials and officers. One of the most notorious of their exploits was the murder in 1979 of eighty-three Alawite cadets at the Artillery School in Aleppo. In 1980, an unsuccessful attempt was made on Assad's life. In retaliation, a large number of Brethren interned in a concentration camp were exterminated in cold blood. In Aleppo in 1980 and in Hama in 1981, forces of the regime descended on Sunni quarters, killing indiscriminately in order to terrorize the population and dissuade it from offering shelter and help to the Brethren. The official terror was not efficacious enough, since an insurrection broke out in February 1982 in Hama, leading the regime to bomb the city from the air and to raze a large part of it, indiscriminately killing thousands of citizens in the process. A conspiratorial and terrorist movement thus met its match in a regime equally conspiratorial and terroristic.

Whatever its origins and inspiration, terrorism in modern Islam is unlikely to prove a flash in the pan. It is one manifestation of the deep dislocation of Islamic society in modern times; of the widespread belief in violent political action, derived in equal measure from European ideologies and from bellicosity vis-à-vis the unbeliever and the heretic which is a feature of traditional Islam; and of the simultaneous prevalence of Muslim regimes which, issuing from conspiracy and coup d'état, are devoid of legitimacy.

The Spread of Islamic Terrorism

P. J. VATIKIOTIS

THE GROWTH OF TERRORISM in and from the Middle East should be considered in the context of several fairly recent developments. The first is the importation of radical revolutionary ideas and the politics of liberation from Europe—that is, the notion of politics as salvation or redemption.

A second, earlier, development was the rise of radical youth movements in the Middle East in the 1930s, especially in Egypt and the Fertile Crescent. It was influenced by European ideas of the organic, fascist, or totalitarian state, and by the traditions of authoritarianism and autocracy associated with the indigenous view of power and the state. These youth movements shared one thing in common: the rejection of the cumbersome process of deliberative politics in favor of violence as the preferred means for the attainment of their political aims. This violence was to be directed against the prevailing order, as well as the representatives of European culture and the dominant Western civilization. It expressed a rejection of imported ideas and institutions as means of coping with the problems of modernity, and a preference for the more native and more familiar system.

The tradition of violence and autocracy spawned the growth of terrorism, whether practiced by individuals, groups, or rulers and states. In the case of the last, one must bear in mind that religion in the Middle East is a potent ideological force which challenges territorial rule. The religion-based identity of Middle

[77]

Easterners has resisted the secular integration of nationalism, and politics itself has been viewed as a variant of religion, if not religion incarnate. The religious and ethnic mosaic of the Middle East has often ignored, and rejected, the national boundaries so recently imposed upon it. Movements of religious reform, nationalism, and constitutionalism attempted without much success to reconcile the beliefs and institutions of an earlier age to the requirements of the modern system of nation-states.

There was no philosophical commitment to secularism and its values of skepticism, experimentation, and tolerance, so essential to pluralistic politics. With one or two exceptions, the states that have arisen in the Middle East are not genuine nation-states. The nation-state's authority is rooted in a specific territorial base and not on universalist, extraterritorial conceptions.

The term nation-state is therefore misleading when applied to many countries in the Middle East. In most of them the nation is considered in religious terms and is seen to encompass people who live beyond and across the territorial boundaries of the individual states. There is a constant clash between the exigencies of the modern territorial state and those of the wider nation or community of believers.

Caught between a tradition that insists on the supremacy of the nation of Islam and the requirements of the modern territorial secular state, governments in the Middle East have found themselves in a dangerous position. Lebanon and Iran, two recent examples, foundered. Failing to construct regimes outside religion, one collapsed into chaos, the other succumbed to the tyranny of a near-medieval fundamentalism. In Lebanon, the territorial rule gave way to sectarian jurisdiction and nationality. In Iran, the dominant Shiite community of believers ignores territorial boundaries and seeks to extend its "universal truth" among fellow believers across national boundaries. Such notions of power and authority based on religion and ideology suggest that throughout the Middle East the legitimization of power is still widely contested and authority is tenuous.

Very often the ruler is the state, since he is not really accountable to a body of elected representatives. Unconstrained Middle Eastern rulers have resorted to terrorism for domestic, regional, and international political purposes. The assumption of power by soldiers and the proliferation of rival military regimes accelerated this trend, which had begun in the 1950s. In radicalizing Arab politics, Nasser used terror against his opponents at home and subversion against his rivals in the region. But he did not attempt international terrorism on a large scale. Nor did he pursue his opponents abroad with a view to liquidating them. This did not occur until the 1970s, when money from oil became more abundant. Iraq, Libya, and South Yemen, for example, pursued their adversaries anywhere in the world. They concentrated on Western Europe, whose power and prestige in the world had declined, and whose open political systems afforded Arab operatives the freedom and impunity of liberal systems. Libya, especially, adopted international terrorism in order to extend the policies of a classical despot.

In the late 1960s the PLO's terrorist attacks against international civil aviation gave a unique impetus to international terrorism. Unable to engage Israel militarily, the PLO assumed that terrorist acts would force the international community to assist it in its cause. These acts were of course intended as blackmail. The only major figure in these activities I have known personally since childhood was the late Wadi Haddad. He acquired great notoriety as the planner of aircraft hijackings, particularly the infamous one at Dawson Field in Amman in 1970. Haddad believed that the West, as much as Israel and Jews throughout the world, was the enemy of the Palestinians. Dramatic and violent action, including terrorism, was in his view what distinguished him and his generation from the supine, passive, collaborative generation of his father.

Is there a connection between religious commitment—specifically, the desire to restore power to the Islamic nation—and terrorism? Is there anything in the political experience of Muslims and the perceptions growing out of Islam which inclines some Muslims toward terrorism?

If those who claim to represent Islam and wish to implement its law reject all other forms of law, if they insist on the necessity of an all-embracing and uniform ideological purity, there is clearly an unbridgeable gap between them and differing social and political conceptions. The dichotomy, in fact, between the Islamic and all other systems of government and authority is clear, sharp, and permanent; it is also marked by hostility. The system of nation-states is basically Western, and the kind of temporal political order it has evolved is un-Islamic. There is, then, nothing unethical or immoral, let alone criminal, in attacking the West's representatives and institutions. In the parlance of the fanatic, *dam al-kafir halal,* spilling the blood of the infidel has God's blessing.

But government use of terrorism for international purposes goes beyond the domestic terrorism of, say, the Muslim Brethren and its offshoots. It goes beyond the bombings and kidnappings of the radical Young Egypt Society or the secret organization of the National Party in the 1930s and 1940s; it goes beyond the assassinations perpetrated by the Mufti's men in Palestine in the period from 1936 to 1945, or even the much earlier terrorism of the original Assassins.

For the Muslim Brethren attacked regimes they disapproved of at home, as well as "alien intruders" in the "domain of Islam," such as the Jews in Palestine and the British in the Suez Canal. They did not, however, extend their activities to indiscriminate international terrorism. Since the early 1950s, they have had, of course, links with other Islamic organizations and their terrorist squads, such as the Jamaa-i Islam in Pakistan and the Fedayan-i Islam in Iran. Recently, they have assumed the leadership of Sunni opposition to the heretical Alawite regime of President Assad in Syria. Elsewhere, they act as a pressure group on governments, forcing them to heed Islamic pressures to modify their rule along more traditional lines. They have received financial assistance from Islamic regimes such as Saudi Arabia. But even their most fanatical splinter groups, such as Shabab Muhammad and Jund Allah in Egypt, confine their terrorism to domestic targets.

Today there are new forces. With abundant funds available, groups such as the PLO and Iranian suicide squads can perpetrate terror at home, in the region, and abroad. Their use by such states as Libya, Iran, Iraq, and Syria against their domestic and foreign opponents has become widespread. Often the justification in the mind of the terrorist himself is that he is combating the "Other," the unbeliever, the infidel. He may even act upon a formal religious dispensation which renders his act a Muslim duty.

Islamic revival has also led to the backing of Muslim communities outside the Middle East. The purpose is to help them assume enough power to govern themselves according to the law of God and thus lead proper Muslim lives. Autonomy movements, rebellions, and uprisings in Thailand, the Philippines, Eritrea, and elsewhere have received financing from Islamic states.

Libya, Syria, Iraq, and Iran have also used the PLO and Islamic militants to attack the representatives of sister regimes and other governments: Syria against Jordanian facilities and diplomats in India, Greece, Italy, and France; Iraq against Syria; Iran against the United States, Israel, Iraq, Saudi Arabia, and the Persian Gulf states; and Libya against the Sudan, Egypt, and other countries.

Thus, while nothing in Islamic doctrine links it specifically to terrorism, there is a general Islamic injunction that power belongs to the believers for use against unbelievers, and that the latter should be fought until the earthly order is established under Allah. At a time of Islam's resurgence, the drive to reinstate its power and authority assumes new importance for the believers. It also serves as the means of revenge against all the injustices, real or imagined, especially those associated with the infidel, dominant West.

The rise in Islamic terrorism is often linked to the euphoric belief that there is an Islamic revival. The rapid and widespread recognition given by the world to an international Islamic identity in recent years, a byproduct of the oil crisis, was paralleled by the decline of Western power and prestige. Muslims everywhere saw the oil boom as a shift of power in their favor and a sign of divine approval. Islamic groups, states, and rulers can justify the use of terrorism with the claim that they are simply accelerating this divinely written shift of power.

Despite the use of terror by Islamic militants in the Middle East and elsewhere, some Middle Eastern regimes are alive to its dangers and try to counter it accordingly. This is especially true of Egypt, Saudi Arabia, and the Persian Gulf states. Though these regimes have had to permit Islamic influence on their institutions and policies, they do not recognize such groups as alternative governments and view them with great hostility and suspicion. Yet given the widespread use of Islamic terms and the lip service paid to an Islamic vision of the world, terrorism in the name of the righteous cause will continue to flourish.

Islamic terrorism has little to commend itself for non-radical, pious Muslims. It is merely an unavoidable offshoot of the historical experience of Islamic political life. Those who resort to domestic and international terrorism anywhere are invariably despotic. The Islamic nexus only provides these particular perpetrators with a justification for terrorism. But the doctrinal conflict between Islam and the non-Islamic world helps in its own way to promote terrorist conflict.

Traditional societies in the Middle East are challenged by the twentieth century. Their accustomed view of man and the universe is at odds with modernity. Passionate traditionalists respond with violence, supported by the consolation of martyrdom. But the influence of modernity will not go away. It will, in fact, increase. And this may invite more violence, more autocracies, more tyrannies.

These reactions are not likely to be confined to the Middle East. Terrorism will breed in the tense expanse from the Indian subcontinent to the Levant, where Islamic minorities frequently live under authoritarian regimes which, even when not repressive, are unable to produce a political arrangement that satisfies them. As they seek autonomy, Muslim populations are prone to challenge the legitimacy of these regimes and attack its structures. This militancy, already present in Southeast Asia, will probably spread from India to the Sudan. It could extend in the future to Turkey and the Soviet Union.

As European influence receded, political liberalism failed to take root in the Middle East. The return of the traditional politics of violence was inevitable. Widespread autocratic rule and interstate rivalries, the brutalizing impact of the upheavals in Lebanon, the bloody Persian Gulf war, all have combined to promote the rule of the gun over the rule of law. For this reason, one cannot separate, in the Middle East, international terrorism from domestic terrorism. In practice, one cannot condemn the one without condemning the other; nor can one combat the one without combating the other.

IV

THE INTERNATIONAL NETWORK

TERRORISM could not have attained its present proportions or its international scope without the support of states and the collaboration between terrorist groups throughout the world. Within most countries, especially those with stable governments and disciplined military and police forces, terrorist groups acting alone simply do not have the means to carry out sustained attacks, or to survive for very long. What enables the terrorist to carry on is, above all, outside support, that is, the support of governments.

To begin with, governments provide all-important sanctuary. A terrorist often can escape capture or punishment simply by slipping across the border; and states friendly to terrorism also provide sanctuary *within* the attacked countries, by making available to terrorists the use of their embassies or safe houses. They also train terrorists, and give them money, weapons, and access to crucial intelligence.

Which governments? *Cui bono?* Who profits? the Romans would ask whenever the perpetrators of an act refused to step forward. In the case of many terrorist attacks perpetrated against the West and its allies in recent years, the answer is quite clear. There is by now overwhelming evidence of the involvement with terrorist groups of the Soviet Union and some of its satellites, especially Cuba, and of the radical Arab states (to which must now be added non-Arab Iran). Often such involvement is indirect, using intermediaries. But governments also practice terrorism directly. Though difficult to trace, the circumstantial evidence can be substantial, as in the involvement of Syria and Iran in the bombings of the American embassies in Lebanon and Kuwait.

Beyond the involvement of states, there have been numerous documented cases of various terrorist groups collaborating with each other, and sometimes proclaiming this to the world: the Japanese Red Army with the PFLP, Italy's Red Brigades with Germany's Baader-Meinhof gang, the Red Army Faction (Baader-Meinhof's successor) with the French Direct Action.

In many such cases, the pivotal link was provided by the PLO, which has been supported in turn by the Soviet Union and the Arab world. Fiercely anti-West, it is committed to assisting "national liberation" struggles from Ireland to Turkey, from Central America to Southeast Asia. For nearly a decade the PLO was the only terrorist group in existence to possess, in Lebanon, a quasi-independent state to which terrorists from all over the world were brought for training and, in many cases, indoctrination. Though the PLO lost its terrorist base in Lebanon, it continues to play through its various factions, its contacts, its funds, and its worldwide operations a pivotal role in international terrorism. Any discussion of the problem must recognize that, however disguised, this network of support by state and terrorist organizations alike not only exists but is fundamental to the terrible effectiveness of modern terrorism.

Soviet Sponsorship:
The Will to Disbelieve

MICHAEL A. LEDEEN

FOR MANY YEARS international terrorism has been the subject
of an ongoing debate in the West. There is disagreement over
virtually every element of the problem, from its very definition
to the proper means and methods to combat it. Some view
terrorism as primarily a domestic issue: international terrorist
connections and collaboration may be an interesting phenomenon, but they are peripheral to the essence of the problem and
its solution. Others have insisted that there is an overall framework, if not a guiding hand, under which terrorist groups in
different countries operate, and that understanding this framework is essential for tackling terrorism.

There is no lack of information on terrorist movements, whatever their political origins—from the Uruguayan Tupamaros to
popularized figures like Carlos, from Japan's Red Army to Turkey's Gray Wolves. There is, however, little good analysis. We
can see our poor understanding at work. Virtually every country
in which terrorism has struck has been unprepared for it, even
after international terrorism became so widespread that few
countries could reasonably expect to escape it.

Take the three most dramatic examples of unpreparedness:
The German intelligence service (BND) had no effective coun-
terterrorist unit during the kidnapping and murder of the in-
dustrialist Hans Martin Schleyer by the Baader-Meinhof gang;

the Italians had none during the murder of Aldo Moro by the Red Brigades; neither did the Portuguese at the time of the murder of Issam Sartawi in 1983 by Arab terrorists. Yet each of these countries had fair warning. None heeded it, acting as if terrorist incidents on its own soil were unrelated to the broader phenomenon of global terrorism; each behaved as if terrorism would not spread to its shores.

The Italian government knew that some right-wing terrorists and Sardinian and Sicilian separatists received substantial funding and other assistance from Libya. Yet it was reluctant to accept the notion that Italian terrorism was part of a larger terrorist movement, and that other governments might seek to destabilize Italy through terror.

Still, some Italians realized that although Italian terrorism was partly inspired by strictly internal problems, it had an international dimension as well. They based this conclusion on a substantial body of circumstantial evidence.

For over half a century Italy has had secret revolutionaries. Although they have operated within the general context of the Italian Communist Party (PCI), they have often been at odds with its official leader. These groups have often had secret links with the Soviet bloc. Italian intelligence officials in the late 1970s, studying cases of left-wing assassins of the immediate postwar period, found that many of them had been trained and recruited in the East (in Yugoslavia prior to the Tito split, and later in Czechoslovakia).

In the late forties, the Volante Rossa, a group eerily resembling the Red Brigades, carried out political assassinations; it organized the Communist Party's security service (including the important task of protecting foreign dignitaries visiting Italy on the party's invitation); it assaulted and assassinated selected enemies. Although its members held PCI cards, they acted with considerable autonomy. When the government cracked down on them, Volante Rossa members fled to Eastern Europe, most notably to Czechoslovakia.

During the early 1950s, the PCI also maintained a covert paramilitary organization. Numbering at least 100,000 armed men, according to National Security Council estimates at the time, it stored weapons in secret caches and trained for the inevitable armed conflict with the capitalist enemy. Its leader was Pietro Secchia, a PCI official nominally in charge of the party's "organization" department. Secchia's clandestine group was classically Soviet, down to such details as the pairing of male and female agents, sometimes in imposed marriage, to prevent infiltration. When Italy appeared on the verge of civil war following the attempted assassination of PCI Secretary-General Palmiro Togliatti in 1948, Secchia's clandestine network surfaced for a few days, occupied central intersections in northern cities, took charge of the national telephone network, and carried out a prearranged military plan, apparently independent of party control.

Secchia was purged in 1953, following a scandal involving one of his top assistants. Significantly, many of his collaborators went to Prague. This is one of the first of many connections between Italian subversives and Czechoslovakia spanning decades. The archives of the PCI were kept in Prague until at least the mid-fifties. PCI couriers regularly carried documents to Prague, and money and instructions back to Italy. In 1968 some twenty-nine Czech and Soviet agents were expelled from Western Europe on information obtained from a Czech agent in Italy. Prague served, in short, as a center for Soviet clandestine operations in Italy, sometimes involving the Communist Party, sometimes not. Years later, many of the original leaders of the Red Brigades went regularly to Prague and maintained contact in Italy with the survivors of the Secchia group. Giangiacomo Feltrinelli, an Italian publisher turned terrorist, went to Czechoslovakia twenty-two times between 1969 and his death in 1972. Carlo Curcio, the first leader of the Red Brigades, went often to Prague, as did his right-hand man, Franceschini.

At a minimum, the founders of left-wing Italian terrorism of the sixties went to Prague to meet people experienced in running a clandestine network in Italy. To Italian security officials this was highly suggestive: if the Russians had operated in Italy through Prague in the past, was it unreasonable to fear that they were doing so again, especially with a movement that bore such striking resemblance to its predecessor?

While evidence of foreign involvement in Italian terrorism of the left was circumstantial, there was hard evidence for such involvement on the right. Italian officials knew that Libya provided money, training, and weapons to neo-Nazi organizations such as Ordine Nero, and to various separatist movements in Sardinia and Sicily (a particular target of Qaddafi's). Since Libya was developing very close ties to the Soviet Union, could this Libyan involvement in Italian terrorism be another Soviet tactic for destabilizing the country?

The notion that terrorism in Italy might be part of a larger effort, with significant Soviet support and possibly control, was supported by four pieces of direct evidence: the terrorist conference of 1972 in Badawi, Lebanon, the PLO's role in international terrorism, and the testimonies of General Jan Sejna and of Ion Mihai Pacepa.

The Badawi Conference on international terrorist movements was organized in 1972 by George Habbash, head of the PFLP branch of the PLO. Most of the leading terrorist groups attended the meeting, which was held in great secrecy in a Palestinian refugee camp outside Tripoli. At its conclusion, Habbash announced: "We have created organic supports between the Palestinians and the revolutionaries of the entire world." In subsequent years, the nature of these "organic supports" became evident in the Middle East and Western Europe. Black September, for example, carried out the firebombing of the oil refineries in Trieste at the request of the Red Brigades, while an extremist cell in Rome was discovered transporting SAM–7 missiles for the PFLP (a connection overt enough for Habbash to send a letter to the Italian court accepting PFLP responsibility and asking for the return of the missiles). Similar ties were revealed with German terrorists from the Baader-Meinhof gang and later the Red Army Faction.

It is especially significant that two high-level officials from the PLO who did not belong to its PFLP faction, Abu Iyad and Fouad Chemali, were present when this formal agreement to aid other terrorist groups was unanimously approved. The international terrorist network could now enjoy the money and connections of the PLO.

The Soviet–PLO connection hardly needs documentation, as PLO leaders have publicly acknowledged that thousands of fedayeen have been trained in the U.S.S.R. The Soviet Union has given PLO operatives special diplomatic status, allowing them easy movement throughout Eastern Europe.

But the most striking direct testimony of Soviet involvement in international terrorism comes from the Czechoslovakian defector General Jan Sejna. Sejna said that he was personally involved in a training program for foreign terrorists in Czechoslovakia under the direct control of Soviet Military Intelligence (the GRU). Sejna provided details of the training and names of Italians who had gone through the program. Included among them were well-known figures in the Red Brigades such as Feltrinelli and Franceschini, and others who were at the time unknown but who subsequently turned out to be important terrorists.

In a document submitted to two parliamentary commissions in 1983, the Italian government said that by 1978 it had compiled a list of Italians believed to have undergone terrorist training in Czechoslovakia. This document also revealed that the terrorist leader Giangiacomo Feltrinelli fled Italy for Czechoslovakia in 1971 in a move that "would have been impossible without Czech security officials' approval . . ."

Additional light on Soviet-bloc connections to Italian terrorism was shed by the information obtained during the investigation of the kidnapping of General James Dozier by the Red Brigades. The investigation revealed that the Red Brigades had discussions with the Bulgarian intelligence service during the kidnapping. To Italian intelligence officials, the "Bulgarian connection" was not an isolated case but part of a decades-old pattern of documented Soviet subversion in Italy. This was not limited to groups on the political left; in the 1960s, for example, a so-called Nazi-Maoist extremist group was created in Italy by the Czechoslovakian intelligence service. When, in the 1980s, it appeared that the Bulgarian service might be working through a right-wing Turkish group, the Gray Wolves, this was far from inconceivable.

Testimony of Soviet and Bulgarian involvement in Italian terrorism came from still another Soviet-bloc defector, Ion Mihai

Pacepa, the former deputy director of the Rumanian intelligence service, who defected to the West in 1978. He told American officials that Red Brigades members had been trained in Bulgaria as recently as the time of the kidnapping and murder of Aldo Moro.

Even without the testimony of defectors like Pacepa and Sejna, there was other firsthand evidence of Russian assistance to terrorists in Europe. In 1974 in Brussels, an automobile carrying two known KGB agents had an "accident" arranged by European security services. Belgian security officials found in the automobile documents describing the headquarters of terrorist operations based in Vienna. This center coordinated operations with terrorist groups ranging from the Red Brigades to the Japanese Red Army in Europe. Within hours of the incident, the Vienna center was shut down and moved to Libya.

Terrorist States

MOSHE ARENS

LIEUTENANT COLONEL JONATHAN NETANYAHU (Yoni) fell while leading the Israeli rescue operation at Entebbe. To all Israelis, but especially to the officers and men of the Israel Defense Forces, he remains alive as an example of leadership, tenacity, and courage. The collection of his letters is widely read by Israeli youth, and the story of Entebbe is told and retold. We in Israel are proud that Yoni's qualities of dedication and readiness for sacrifice are so cherished by Israel's young people. And to the world, Yoni has become a symbol of resistance to terror, an object lesson that terror can be defeated.

But it cannot be defeated with defensive measures alone. Preventive measures, good preparation, and good intelligence are not enough. We must recognize that we are in a state of war, an undeclared and broad war, a war against Western society. To force ourselves into a defensive posture, to exclude the option of taking the offensive, is as suicidal in the case of terrorism as it would be in any other form of warfare.

Israel lived with terrorism even before it became a state. Terrorism has been a means by which our enemies, supported by the Nazis in the 1930s and by the Soviets since the 1960s, have hoped to eliminate us. The PLO, the umbrella organization of virtually all Arab terrorist groups, was established in 1964, three years *before* the 1967 Six-Day War and before Israeli control over Judea and Samaria became an issue. For the goal of the PLO was then, and is now, not the retrieval of the so-called occupied territories, but the destruction of Israel whatever its borders. With the support of the Arab states and the Soviet Union, the PLO grew to awesome proportions. By June 1982 there were about 15,500 armed PLO terrorists in Lebanon.

They amassed vast quantities of weapons, including 130 mm guns and Soviet B–21 rocket launchers, as well as T–34 and T–54 tanks. This heavy weaponry provided them with the capability of shelling Israeli towns and settlements in the Galilee with relative impunity. About 6,000 tons of ammunition and 50,000 pieces of light weaponry were discovered in PLO arsenals in Lebanon by the Israel Defense Forces. The PLO "state" had its own airport at Beirut and its own harbors at Tyre and Sidon.

The intolerable threat to the safety of every man, woman, and child living in the Galilee was removed by the Peace for Galilee Operation. But by striking a lethal blow to the PLO power base, the operation also benefited all who were likely to become the targets of international terrorism. For in 1981–82 alone, the PLO trained close to one thousand foreign terrorists in Lebanon. Several meetings of international terrorists were held in Beirut under PLO auspices. The last such meeting, in November 1981, included the Japanese Red Army, the Polisario group, and the Red Brigades. Had the nations of the free world, instead of criticizing Israel, fully supported its actions in Lebanon, the PLO would have been eliminated as a threat to Israel and to the other democratic countries.

The PLO, however, is not alone in fostering international terror. A number of Middle Eastern states have adopted terror as a principal method of warfare. There are five such terrorist states in the Middle East—Iraq, Libya, Syria, South Yemen, and Iran—and they share some common features: all are autocratic regimes; all, with the exception of Iran, have close ties with the Soviet Union and receive most of their arms from it; and all are deeply anti-Western. Without their active support and initiation, the waves of international terrorism in recent years would not have been possible.

The outstanding example of Iraq's assistance to terrorism is the June 1982 attempted murder of Israeli Ambassador Shlomo

Argov in London. Iraq's intelligence services provided the documents, weapons, and apparently also the planning for the Abu Nidal faction. This same group carried out attacks on Iraq's behalf against Syrian, Iranian, and other Israeli targets. But Iraq did not confine its support for terrorists to the Abu Nidal group. We know with certainty that in 1979 it provided training facilities for extremist leftist groups from Europe. The need to turn to the West for weapons and credits as a result of its war with Iran has forced Iraq to abandon for now terrorist activities in the West. But given the record and nature of the regime in Baghdad it is difficult to see this as much more than a temporary tactic.

Libya under Qaddafi, of course, has broken all records in the methodical use of terror and subversion. Since Qaddafi's takeover in 1969, Libya has supported most of the terrorist groups throughout the world. It has served as a haven for many international terrorists. Murderers and hijackers of airplanes have been received in Libya as heroes. There are more than twenty Libyan training camps for terrorists of various nationalities (factions of the PLO, various African organizations such as SWAPO and Polisario, the IRA and the Red Brigades, to name a few). Libyan embassies transfer arms and provide documents and diplomatic cover for terrorists.

Syrian-sponsored terrorism is directed against the United States, Israel, Western Europe, Arab countries not aligned with Syria, and Syrian groups opposed to the present regime. Syria's terrorism is carried out by Palestinian Arab terrorist organizations, and its own intelligence apparatus with agents in Syrian embassies worldwide. But Syria has also recruited the services of non-Arab terrorist organizations, such as the Armenian Liberation Organization, the Japanese Red Army, and the Patani Liberation Organization of Thailand, all of whose representatives sit permanently in Damascus.

Some of the better-known acts of Syrian-backed terror include the Shiite bombing of the American embassy in Beirut in April 1983 and the October 1983 bombing of the Marines and French headquarters in Beirut. Syria has also used terrorism to warn Jordan's King Hussein not to make any independent political moves; in 1983 it ordered the Abu Nidal faction to carry out a series of attacks on Jordanian government facilities in Amman. This is in character with Syria's manner of dealing with dissent from without and within. In February 1982, Syria's armed forces killed more than 20,000 civilians in the Syrian city of Hama. Syria has since carried out countless assassinations and other acts of terrorism in and from chaotic Lebanon.

In recent years, Iran has emerged as a major force in the exportation of terror. The Iranian regime views terrorism as a legitimate tool for exporting the Islamic revolution, that is, of achieving the "liberation" of Muslims in general and of Shiite communities in particular. The main targets of Iranian terrorism are America and Israel. But there are others: states defined as "reactionary" and "imperialist," the sheikdoms of the Persian Gulf, Iraq, Saudi Arabia, and even countries such as the Philippines and Sri Lanka—in short, all those opposed to the Khomeini regime or believed to be derelict in adhering to its vision of Islam.

Finally, South Yemen has provided facilities to terrorists from around the world and actively cooperates with Libya. Some of the most infamous terrorist acts of the last two decades may be traced to this backward regime, and many of the world's most active terrorists have found refuge there at one time or another.

Clearly, a purely defensive approach will not succeed in countering this multitentacled monster, which threatens not only Israel, or the Middle East, but the entire free world. Vigilance, preparedness, intelligence, and other defensive efforts are obviously essential. But more is needed. Aggressive unequivocal steps have to be taken by *all* the democracies, including the following:

First, the PLO has offices in many countries throughout the world. They are used for disseminating propaganda in favor of terrorism and as centers for terrorist acts. These offices have in many cases been granted the status of diplomatic missions. If terrorism is to be fought effectively, the offices must be closed.

Second, the free nations should jointly warn the governments of Libya, Syria, Iraq, South Yemen, and Iran, or any other government supporting terrorists, that shielding terrorism behind the façade and immunity of their embassies will no longer be tolerated.

Third, since terrorism can strike swiftly and unexpectedly anywhere on the globe, the democracies should arrive at a common agreement for collaboration among their military forces. This will facilitate launching operations against terrorists in crises arising from terrorist attacks.

Until these steps are taken, the international effort to combat terrorism will be no more than halfhearted and ineffective. Once they are taken, they will signal our resolve to take the offensive against international terrorism, and our unshakable determination to eliminate it from the face of the earth.

The Centrality of the PLO

JILLIAN BECKER

IN JANUARY 1973, the PLO openly published its intention to actively aid and seek aid from "revolutionary" movements: "Mutual solidarity and support between the Arab national struggle and the world revolutionary struggle are a necessity . . . The Arab Palestinian national struggle is decisively and firmly on the side of the unity of all world revolutionary forces."

By 1976 southern Lebanon had fallen under the rule of the PLO. Except for a small pocket held by the forces of Major Saad Haddad, the PLO had established a territorial base from West Beirut southward. It became the center not only for operations against Israel but for international terrorism as well.

During the 1970s, the PLO mini-state in Lebanon functioned as a center for training and arming subversive organizations from most of the non-communist countries. To the Soviet Union such groups were the potential nuclei of future mass movements, as well as the disrupters of the present order.

It has been known for some time that the Soviet Union uses the PLO as a conduit to aid the terrorist groups of the Western world. Virtually all terrorist groups have received some measure of Soviet aid, though few got it directly by training in the Soviet Union. It was always assumed, however, that the Soviet Union simply allowed itself to be approached by a newly formed terrorist group, and if it felt that the group was usable, it would then support it. PLO documents captured by the Israelis in 1982 prove differently. One such document shows that the Soviet Union, through the PLO, *actively sought out* groups of malcontents and rebels; as they put it, "groups which could be utilized."

It was thus largely because of the PLO that the 1970s was a decade of terrorism. The PLO had resources, control of territory (which included a metropolitan capital), and a special status granted by the U.S.S.R. as the undisputed leader of national liberation movements. The PLO leadership maintained close, almost daily, contact with the Soviet embassy in Beirut. With PLO help, terrorist groups became sufficiently well equipped and trained to constitute a real threat to African and Latin American states, and to disturb most of the liberal democracies.

Ostensibly stateless, Palestinians who were members of the PLO could travel abroad without difficulty. The El Fatah branch of the PLO could, and often did, issue passports in the name of Arab states, grant visa permits for those states, and use their stamps. PLO leaders were involved in terrorist attacks carried out by non-Arab groups outside the Middle East.

On June 27, 1976, two German terrorists helped the PLO hijack a French airplane to Uganda, whose dictator, Idi Amin, colluded with the PLO. The plan of the hijacking was conceived by Wadi Haddad. It ended in failure when Israeli commandos stormed the airfield at Entebbe and rescued the hostages. Yet this was not the last publicly known case of cooperation between Arab and West German terrorists. On October 13, 1977, a German plane flying from Majorca was hijacked by four Arabs to Mogadishu in Somalia. The hijackers demanded the release of eleven German terrorists from West German jails. Here, too, the hijacking was foiled, this time by West German forces. At the time, Wadi Haddad, whose group had carried out this hijacking as well, was lying ill in an East German hospital. As far as is known, no pressure was brought to bear on him to call off the operation.

Documents captured during Israel's action in Lebanon in 1982 showed that terrorists from West Germany, Italy, Northern Ireland, Spain, Holland, France, Turkey, Greece, Cyprus, Japan, Argentina, East Timor, Eritrea, the United States, Chile, and southern Africa visited PLO camps in Lebanon. These foreign terrorists were trained in several centers. Basque, German, and Italian terrorists were trained in Shatilla. Over one hundred Spanish terrorists were trained at Burj al-Barajneh in Beirut in 1979 (as well as in Hamariyah in Syria). The Turkish Gray Wolves were the first foreign terrorist group to go to the PLO in Lebanon for training. Several of its members were found in the Palestinian camp of Tal al-Za'tar in the 1960s, where they were later joined by Cubans, Somalians, and Pakistanis.

The Christian town of Damur, once with a population of 25,000 people, was entirely sacked. In one night in January 1976, the PLO killed 582 of its residents, and the rest fled. Like other towns in PLO-controlled Lebanon, Damur was turned into a gathering place of international terrorists. In 1982 I found documents indicating that the Gray Wolves had kept an office there. Fewer than 200 yards away there were similar traces of ASALA, the Armenian Secret Army for the Liberation of Armenia.

The association between the PLO and European groups produced a series of terrorist attacks in Europe. In October 1979 a synagogue was attacked in the rue Copernic in Paris by French collaborators of the PLO. In 1980 two mass bombings, one at a railway station in Bologna, the other at Munich, were carried out by Germans and Italians working closely with the PLO.

Swedes, Norwegians, and Danes also found their way to the camps, some for humanitarian reasons, but not all. For example, two Norwegians captured by Israel in 1982 were active supporters of the PLO. The PFLP counted Swedes and Norwegians among its active members.

Fugitive terrorists were given asylum in Beirut, usually in Shatilla. Several members of the German Red Army Faction were given shelter and false documents. At least forty-five members of the IRA were known to have found asylum with the PLO. Thomas MacMahon, convicted for the murder of Lord Mountbatten in 1979, was trained in a PFLP camp.

Foreign terrorists entered Lebanon either through Syria or, increasingly, through Beirut airport. From the late 1960s the PLO competed with the Lebanese government to allow foreign terrorists to enter Lebanon without the usual immigration procedures. A daily list of PLO visitors was handed to the passport and customs authorities. Some of the visitors went to the camps for training, others were lodged in PLO apartment buildings in West Beirut, on or near the fashionable shopping street of Hamra. There were also special hotels for PLO guests and friends: the Commodore, where the foreign correspondents gathered; the Plaza; and several others. The whole of West Beirut was under PLO control.

PLO "special baggage," containing weapons, explosives, and grenades, left Beirut daily on Middle East Airlines flights. Lebanese authorities could not interfere. Among the employees of every airline, including those of Europe and the United States, were hostesses or stewards bribed with monthly payments by the PLO who made sure that this "special baggage," disguised as diplomatic bags, got through without difficulty at ports of entry.

On the few occasions when the Lebanese government protested, such as when the PLO brought in a group of Iranians in January 1980, the PLO simply ignored the objections.

The daily airport list of the PLO usually had twenty to fifty names on it. This means that thousands of people came to the PLO's mini-state in South Lebanon. Many were cultivated as friends of the PLO. Many more were trained, armed, and indoctrinated. They were regularly put in touch with the Soviet Union's embassy in West Beirut.

And they were given a license to satisfy their instinct to kill. In the civil war in Beirut in 1975 and 1976, they would perch on balconies and rooftops and shoot down into the streets at anyone. They often could not even see whom they were shooting at. I have pictures of people shot in bars, in armchairs, on their doorsteps; of a man who found his dead son in the street and dragged his body home; of children shot with their pet animals.

These terrorists, what I call the "fun revolutionaries" from Europe, and their mercenary colleagues from all over the world could come to Lebanon, receive a Kalashnikov rifle, and "experience the thrill" of killing people. They could then leave with impunity, return to their safe lives in their safe societies, and live like any normal citizen. They will never have to answer for the crimes they committed in Lebanon.

The disintegration of the PLO since its expulsion by Israel from Lebanon might have been expected to bring about a significant reduction in terrorist activity. This has not happened because certain states continue to shelter terrorists and encourage them to act abroad. The PLO, weakened and splintered, is thus still able to foment terror, though not on the scale it was once accustomed to from its now defunct terrorist empire in Lebanon.

Unraveling the Riddle

CLAIRE STERLING

THE ATTACK on Pope John Paul II was an attempt to assassinate a public figure by a state secret service under the guise of a right-wing terrorist action. The world had become so inured to terrorism that this was the most acceptable method by which the Soviet Union could physically eliminate the Polish Pope, whom it came to regard as a political threat.

What is interesting about this case is not only that it was planned to be accepted as such but that an existing European terrorist group was actually recruited for the services it could provide. These details were not widely known initially. Only the Italian investigating magistrate was able to see them clearly as his inquiry progressed over three years.

Despite Agca's erratic performance in the courtroom—deliberately erratic to advance his strategy for getting out of jail—the evidence indicates overwhelmingly that the Soviets had decided, probably within the Politburo, that Pope John Paul had to go. They then assigned the task to Bulgaria, which in turn commissioned the Turkish Mafia, a criminal band subsidized, sponsored, and directed by the Bulgarian security service. The Bulgarians directed the Turkish Mafia to recruit one of its professional killers, Mehmet Ali Agca, for the actual shooting of the Pope. In a meeting with an agent of the Bulgarian Secret Service DS (the treasurer of the Bulgarian embassy in Rome), it was agreed that Bulgaria would put up the money, provide the escape

route by means of an international truck, and arrange for sanctuary.

The operational plans would be entrusted to Agca and his
close friend and accomplice Oral Celik, both associated with the
right-wing terrorist Gray Wolves in Turkey. Agca had already
achieved notoriety as a convicted murderer of a newspaper editor
in Turkey. He and Celik were to use the Gray Wolves' contacts
in Western Europe for safe houses, cash, weapons, and intelligence until the plot could be carried out.

These are the elements of what we call the "terror network."
It has become a useful means by which the Soviet Union and
its clients try to destabilize Western European countries.

The question is not whether a small group can paralyze Italy
for considerable periods. That has already been clearly demonstrated by the terror campaign waged by the Red Brigades.
Other terrorist groups showed a similar capacity in West Germany, Spain, and Northern Ireland, and have actually toppled
a democratic government in Turkey. The world now accepts that
terrorist groups can do all that, and is no longer shocked by it.

But as this case shows, terrorists can be used for purposes
even more sinister than destabilization. If a particular adversary
in the West is undesirable, the Soviets can use terrorists to
eliminate him.

One of the most striking things about the papal assassination
case is the hostile skepticism in the West toward the view that
the Bulgarian (and Soviet) services were involved, despite evidence presented by the Italian state prosecutor. The skeptics,
for example, asked why the three Bulgarians stayed in Rome so
long after the assassination attempt. The initial assumption was
that only one of them, Antonov, stayed around until he was
arrested, while the others had cleared out earlier. In fact, all
three Bulgarian agents accused of organizing the conspiracy stayed
in Rome for some time. One did not leave until fifteen months
after the Pope was shot (ten days after my first article about the
Bulgarian connection appeared in *The Reader's Digest*). Another
did not leave until the investigating judge, Ilario Martella, began
to inquire into his diplomatic immunity. He left the next day.

Antonov was the only one who did not get out in time and was caught.

Why did the Bulgarians stay so long? One reason might have been that they were convinced that even if an Italian judge were put on the case, either he would not have the courage to proceed or he would be discouraged from doing so. The government of Italy, and the West in general, would have little interest in exposing this plot because of a deeply ingrained reluctance to confront the Soviet Union. The disposition would be to ignore and cover up.

Indeed, within two days of the shooting, a leading American newspaper reported that officials of the Italian government believed that Agca had acted alone, despite the fact that the magistrates had already said: "We have evidence that this man, Agca, did not act alone."

But as the evidence began to come in, skepticism gave way to stunned silence. Until then the idea of Soviet involvement was dismissed as impossible because, as so many Western intelligence services would assure anybody who asked, the Russians were far too cautious, far too careful, far too efficient to have made such a miscalculation.

If the silence has been broken, it is not because of a change of attitude in the Western establishment. It is because an Italian judge, contrary to the arrogant assumptions of the Soviets and the Bulgarians, had the courage and the integrity to proceed with the investigation, and pursue it to its conclusion. Regardless of the outcome of the trial, in which the star witness never retracted his confession implicating the Bulgarians, but did everything in his power to destroy his own credibility, the historic truth has already been established by the work of the Italian judiciary. How can a free society begin to defend itself against terrorism? The example given by the Italian magistrate is a good start.

Japan's Terror Groups

TAKESHI MURAMATSU

ANY DEMOCRATIC SOCIETY is vulnerable to assault from those who seek to impose their will by violence. Plato said that democracy will always produce dissidents who will disrupt the peace for their own ends; even if caught and sentenced, they will reappear again as phantoms.

Japan has such phantoms, organized in many groups. Of these, three engage in terrorist activities abroad. The first and oldest is the Red Army, whose base is believed to be in Baalbek, Lebanon. The second is a group controlled by North Korea that fled to Pyongyang in 1970 after hijacking a plane. The third organization, which appeared in 1984 in Paris, bombing the Sony and Mitsubishi buildings there, called itself the Japanese Anarchists. Although some believe that it is in fact the Japanese Red Army, the relationship between the two groups has not been firmly established.

Of these three groups, the Red Army is clearly the most important. A Red Army member named Shigenobu was interviewed in Baalbek by a newsman sympathetic to the PLO. She said that the size of the Red Army was greater than was generally estimated, and that during the Israeli action in Lebanon in 1982, members of the Red Army fought alongside the PLO in Nabatiyeh, Halde, and Beaufort Castle. Japanese police, in fact, say that the Red Army often sends appeals to the Japanese public. It obtains information about the political situation in Japan, especially on the left, through supporters in Paris and the West Coast of the United States. It is also possible that the Red Army has recruited new members in Japan and abroad.

The Japanese Red Army was originally organized under Wadi Haddad of the PFLP in 1971 under the name Arab Committee of the Red Army. By 1974, however, it was increasingly autonomous from the PFLP. When it took over the French embassy in the Netherlands in 1974, no Arab terrorists were involved. And the terrorists who hijacked a Japan Air Lines jetliner in Dacca in 1977 were all Japanese. This independence from direct Arab influence came to an end when the Iran-Iraq war began. With an eye to the West and the Gulf States, Saddam Hussein decided to expel from Iraq the Japanese Red Army and most other terrorist groups, leaving at that time only Abu Nidal's group. (Abu Nidal quickly found new havens, first in Syria, then in Libya.) The Japanese Red Army now found itself obliged to work under the umbrella of the PLO in Lebanon, where it established new headquarters, or risk losing its new center in Hebania. In 1981 it began to issue a bi-weekly magazine entitled in English *Solidarity*, emphasizing, appropriately enough, its solidarity with Arab terrorists. The magazine stressed the need for cooperation with the PLO and the formation of a unified anti-imperialist front, which would include the Soviet Union.

Although all three Japanese terror groups are based abroad, the PLO has sought to foster extreme-left groups within Japan itself. Since the oil crisis of 1973 it has used oil as a political weapon. The Japanese business community was singularly weak in the face of Arab economic threats, and contributed huge sums as a payoff to the Tokyo branch of the PLO. (When a Tokyo-based member of the PLO was told he was being transferred, he accepted his orders with the greatest reluctance; though he sent a portion of his enormous receipts to PLO headquarters, it is said that he was still making a fortune on the side.)

How can the Japanese government help counter worldwide terrorism? It can begin by convincing Japanese businessmen that their contributions to the PLO finance international terrorism. The government should also join in creating an international organization to defend the free world against terrorism. If it does not take these and other measures against terrorism, Japanese democracy could be undermined. There are about 35,000 extreme leftists in Japan in various factions. Though the Red Army in Japan itself is small (its membership is estimated at 150), other organizations, now inert, could be considered "terrorist reserves," easily activated by either the U.S.S.R. or North Korea.

Japan has so far succeeded in maintaining public order, but there are several reasons why a spark of violent terrorism could seriously threaten this calm. As an island nation, Japan has no border to defend against a neighbor. As a result, there is no strong sense of external enemies in Japan. When enemies of democracy present themselves as "freedom fighters," most Japanese do not recognize the threat they pose. Many tend to view terrorists as underdogs, especially if the police take action against them. This sympathy may be rooted in an aversion to the authoritarianism of prewar Japan. It is further compounded by the mass media; Japanese journalists are often sympathetic to people who call themselves opposition fighters, freedom fighters, anarchists, or anti-imperialists. If terrorism should strike hard in Japan, these tendencies might affect public opinion negatively. The vulnerability of democracy which Plato noted some 2,500 years ago is very much evident in the isolated mass society that Japan is today.

V

TERRORISM AND THE MEDIA

THE CHINESE SAYING "Kill one, frighten ten thousand" is applicable to terrorism for obvious reasons. Today's terrorists, in fact, frighten not thousands but millions. But they could not achieve this result without the free press. Unreported, terrorist acts would be like the proverbial tree falling in the silent forest. Even if passed by word of mouth, news about terrorist outrages would hardly command the attention of government leaders, the public at large, and indeed, as often happens, the center of the international stage.

The press has become the unwilling—and in some cases, willing—amplifier of the terrorists' publicity campaign. In free societies much of this is unavoidable, although the pernicious effects of unrestrained coverage can be curbed if the press would exercise toward terrorism the same discretion it applies to coverage of pornography and excessively deviant behavior.

But there is a second, and more fundamental, way in which the world's free press assists the terrorists. It often adopts their terminology and arguments and transmits them to the public uncritically, even sympathetically. Thus the term "guerrillas" (irregular forces that confine their attacks to military targets) is used by the press interchangeably with "terrorists" (who wherever possible attack civilians and non-combatants). Further, the press interviews terrorist murderers, according them the legitimacy of respectable politicians. This is especially deplorable during an actual hostage-taking, when journalists rush to offer terrorists a world forum for well-rehearsed "impromptu" press conferences with numb hostages. In these and other ways the Western media have facilitated the spread of the terrorists' message and have contributed to the confusion in the public mind about their nature and their goal.

How, then, should the press cover terrorism? "If the purpose of terror is to send a message," one American journalist noted, "we messengers should consider not sending it . . . We should publish or broadcast minimal, cool, factual reports, enough to register the event but not enough to set up the society-wide vibrations which the terrorist craves."

In free societies, the real question is not one of censorship but one of self-discipline. Given terrorism's unique dependence on publicity, the authority and power of the Western media entail an obligation for responsible, restrained, and critical reporting of terrorism and its practitioners. It is one thing to ensure that conflicting points of view within a society get a fair hearing. It is another to offer uninhibited access to mass communications to the very forces that are committed to the destruction of free society itself and, not incidentally, its free press.

Partners in Crime

CHARLES KRAUTHAMMER

MODERN TERRORISM differs in several important ways from its immediate predecessor, the classical terrorism practiced by the FLN in Algeria or the Viet Cong in Vietnam. It differs in context, objective, and, most important, in intended audience. FLN terrorism occurred in the context of a real war; its objective was to terrorize, and thus demoralize, the other side; and its audience was the victim, his class and compatriots.

Compare that with the quintessential post-1968 acts of terrorism, the airplane hijackings by the PLO, or its *reductio ad absurdum*, the train hijacking by the Dutch Moluccans. First, these were violent acts that occurred in the total absence of any military confrontation. To compensate, the act was often dressed up in the trappings of war (hence the "communiqué"). For such terrorists war is an aspiration only.

Second, the chief object was not to demoralize but to publicize. The PLO seized planes not merely to spread fear but also to spread its name and its cause. Some terrorists, in fact, make publicity their sole objective, as in the case of the Croatians who seized Yugoslav hostages and demanded only that the press publish their manifesto. Terrorism becomes a form of political advertising. But since the outlaws cannot buy television time, they have to earn it. Like the early television sponsors who actually supplied the drama in order to be able to show their commercials, the media terrorists supply an even more enticing drama—

murder and kidnapping, live—also in return for advertising time.

The third and most important distinction between classical and media terrorism is the intended audience. When the FLN blew up a bar in Algiers, its audience was the victims, the *"pieds noirs."* The PLO hijackings were addressed not to the victims, not even to the enemy, Israel, but to the world. This kind of terrorist act has no intrinsic military purpose, often not even a symbolic purpose. It is the occasion, the lure, the entertainment which earns the terrorist access to the world. And to reach the world, the mass media are absolutely indispensable.

The media are not totally at fault. They do what comes naturally, covering the unusual, the dramatic; and the new terrorist exploits this to get his message out. It is he that makes the media a partner in crime. Often, the media cannot help being enlisted. At Munich, for example, the cameras were already there. It is not as if the media went out in search of terrorist activity.

But only up to a point can the media claim to be unwitting accomplices. After a while one expects them to acquire some sense. They cannot forever plead ignorance. In physics, the Heisenberg principle implies that reality is changed when observed. In politics, the media's effect on terrorism is beyond Heisenberg: observation can actually create the event. Television undoubtedly exacerbated, even prolonged, the Iranian hostage crisis. It managed to turn the American embassy into a television stage. The Iranians had merely to appear on it in order to impose any message they wanted on the world.

If the media are an absolutely intrinsic part of this kind of terrorism, what can be done? I have two modest proposals. First, an exercise of discipline, a willingness to avert one's eyes, self-censorship, if you will. Most in the media are too sophisticated to argue that all they are doing is reporting the news, as if there is an objective world that exists out there and they are simply instruments for bringing it to us. Any honest or sentient newsman knows that an extraordinary exercise of choice and judgment goes into the decision to put Sabra and Shatilla on page 1, while consigning the massacres of the Druse and Shiites a year later to page 20. One is not asking the media to ignore terrorism, simply not to celebrate it. They can report the occurrence of political theater without disseminating the production, through the intelligent exercise of some restraint. In other words, no free rides on the airwaves for terrorists, no matter how creative, how entertaining their crime.

Nor is self-restraint the enemy of press freedom. After all, we restrain many forms of expression. Libel, pornography, race hatred are not permitted on television. Why political murder or mass kidnappings?

Yet it must be admitted that, even with the best intentions, the most intelligent restraint will not abolish media terrorism. The media's business is to cover; some thugs will always find a way to get covered. Hence the second modest proposal: since the media cannot totally prevent themselves from being used by terrorists, they should at least avoid rationalizing or apologizing for them.

Classical terrorism used to be rationalized on the grounds of *military* necessity. It was said that one was justified in hurling grenades at unarmed civilians as a means of waging war against technologically superior foes. Algerian, Vietnamese, and other terrorists justified their use of deliberate civilian killings as a repugnant but necessary means of winning an armed struggle. In the late sixties, terrorism was rationalized on the grounds of *political* necessity. An oppressed and neglected minority had to get its message out. By 1979, a mindless act such as a rocket attack on the American embassy in Beirut, which had no military or political purpose, was passed off as a *psychological* necessity. This is perhaps a vulgarization of Sartre's already vulgar, and notorious, defense of FLN terrorism as an existential necessity. He defended the killing of Europeans as an authentic and essential act of liberation (to which Michael Walzer made the withering retort that if the only way for every Algerian to liberate himself was to kill a European, then the total liberation of Algeria would require the importation of vast numbers of Frenchmen).

And if avoiding apology is too much, at least refrain from romance. One can start by refusing to grant to terrorists, that is, anyone who murders innocents, the honor of the title of guerrilla, or commando, or even fighter. And if the word "terrorist" sounds too loaded, perhaps the press could content itself with a simpler one: murderer.

The Encouragement of Violence

DANIEL SCHORR

AN UNFORTUNATE symbiotic relationship exists between terrorism and television. It was shown in satiric form in the film *Network*, in which a gang of terrorists in effect engaged in paid programming for television, and in a television drama in which Charleston, South Carolina, was destroyed in the interplay between a television station and terrorists.

In real life, television responds to violence, and that encourages further violence. The head of the State Department's Office for Combating Terrorism once associated the increase in casualties during hijackings and hostage-takings with the desire of terrorists to ensure media attention. Deliberate acts of horror, like the tossing out of slain victims, are planned as media events.

Sometimes the aim of terrorists is to hijack television itself. When the Baader-Meinhof gang in West Germany kidnapped a politician in 1975 and held him hostage for the release of five imprisoned comrades, it forced German television to show each released prisoner boarding a plane and to broadcast dictated propaganda statements. "For seventy-two hours we lost control of our medium," said a German television executive. And when Arab terrorists seized the Vienna headquarters of OPEC in 1975, the terrorists' plan called for them to occupy the building until TV cameras arrived.

A central feature of the plan of the Symbionese Liberation Army, which kidnapped Patricia Hearst, was the exploitation of the media. The terrorists forced radio and television to play its tapes and carry its messages. The Hanafi Muslims' hostage-taking occupation of three locations in Washington in 1976 was a classic case of media-age terrorism. The leader, Hamaas Abdul Khalis, spent much of his time giving interviews by telephone while his wife checked what was being broadcast.

Television rewards violence with notoriety, conferring a sense of identity on those seeking to validate their existence. This is as true of terrorists as it is true of other types of criminals. Take three examples of criminals commandeering television: In 1977 in Indianapolis, Anthony Kiritsis wired a sawed-off shotgun to the neck of a mortgage company officer, led him out in front of the TV cameras, and yelled, "Get those goddamn cameras on! I'm a goddamn national hero!"

John Hinckley, Jr., who shot President Reagan, told examining psychiatrists that he had deliberately planned an assassination before news cameras to win maximum media attention. "No crime carries as much publicity as the assassination of the President of the United States," he said. Hinckley's first question to the Secret Service officer who interrogated him was "Is it on TV?" As television again and again, remorselessly, hypnotically, played the videotape of the shooting, the Secret Service recorded an astonishing number of further threats against the President. Hinckley told psychiatrists that he would spend the rest of his life in the spotlight. He had gone, he said, from "obscurity to notoriety." In a speech he wrote for a sentencing which he never got (having been found innocent by reason of insanity), he said, "The entire civilized world knows who I am."

The Washington Monument siege in December 1982 was also apparently planned as a media event to protest the arms race. Norman Mayer made it clear that he wanted to negotiate not with the police but with the media for air time. He apparently spent part of the last day of his life watching from his van the live television coverage of the police siege that was for him his great triumph. It may have been only a coincidence that it was 7:30 P.M., as the network news ended, that Mayer's van started toward the White House to stage the next episode, only to be met with a hail of police fire. One can only speculate whether he would be alive had there been less live coverage. Television thus offers a perverse incentive to the unstable and the fanatical. Because television goes to town on a hostage crisis, some are encouraged to plot hostage crises.

Television is reluctant to confront the unintended consequences of the temptations it offers. But sooner or later it will have to confront the question how to draw a line between responsible coverage and exploitation by terrorists, and whether a hostage incident should be allowed round-the-clock live coverage, complete with ego-satisfying telephone interviews with the terrorists.

Television has come, in some respects, to replace government as an authority figure. It confers prestige and identity. It must learn the responsibility that goes with its influence. That means not encouraging terrorists by giving them the rewards of massive notoriety.

Censorship by Omission

ARNAUD DE BORCHGRAVE

A PERNICIOUS FORM of disinformation about terrorism is censorship by omission. Stories are buried in the inside pages of newspapers because they do not conform to the perception of editors and reporters who mold opinion. One such buried story has been the links between the Soviet bloc and radical Middle Eastern regimes with international terrorists. Though Andrei Sakharov urged us to pay attention to these links, this story has been denigrated by the media as unsubstantiated hearsay.

I have personal experience with censorship by omission. In May 1978 I saw a top-secret French intelligence report which documented in detail the links between the Cuban intelligence service (DGI) and various Western European terrorist groups. The introductory paragraph of this report read:

> The analysis of intelligence collected since 1972 establishes the international solidarity of revolutionary movements in different countries. The terrorist activity of some of them stems from the Tri-Continental Conference held in Havana in January 1966. By 1972 the structures of this terrorist international became operational. The mother cell was in Cuba at the headquarters of the Tri-Continental Organization of People's Solidarity, which the Soviets control through the Cuban secret service. This center coordinates the actions of various "anti-imperialist" movements in the Third World, as well as European terrorist groups, which are for the most part made up of networks that the KGB and its proxy services have established abroad . . .

The report went on to cite names, dates, and places, including houses and training camps. But the story I wrote was killed. It simply did not fit the conventional wisdom of the editors, who could not believe that these things went on in the era of détente.

My associates and I spent almost two years researching the Cuban DGI and its clandestine connections with narcotics in the United States and with international terrorism. In 1982 we wrote a series of articles on what we had learned from Cuban DGI defectors and Latin American, European, and American intelligence services. Two national news syndicates declined to use the series, saying it was not the kind of material their editors or clients would be interested in.

Few people in the media or in academia understand the indirect war now waged by the Soviet Union and its allies. The Soviets have been exceedingly skillful in pursuing, by all means short of outright war, objectives traditionally pursued on the battlefield. Terrorism, along with subversion and disinformation, is a principal weapon directed at societies which the Soviets wish to undermine, chief among which, as KGB documents emphasize, remains the United States.

Terrorism, not nuclear war, is the immediate threat. The spectacular bombings in Beirut against the peacekeepers and against the U.S. embassy started the unraveling of the Western presence in Lebanon. Yet the considerable media coverage these cases received remains an exception. Many crucial facts about international terrorism have been ignored by our media. To cite a few:

A 1983 trial in the Italian city of Trent established Bulgaria's involvement with a lucrative guns-for-heroin ring based in Sofia and supervised by the Bulgarian Secret Service under the control of the KGB. Heroin sales in Western Europe, after all, financed arms purchases for the PLO, as well as for Turkish terrorists across the political spectrum. The trial, and the evidence it produced, was not considered a story worth major media coverage.

In February 1983 a federal trial in Miami established with certainty a Cuban guns-for-drugs connection. This, too, was treated as a non-story. Would the media have ignored the story if Chile's

President Pinochet were involved in American drug traffic and had used the profits to ship guns to right-wing groups in El Salvador? Yet this is precisely what Castro has been up to in this country.

Libya's state-sponsored terrorism has received considerable coverage, but many of its international connections are seldom if ever mentioned. Since 1974, for example, the Libyan Secret Service has been in intimate contact with its East German counterpart, the MFS. In May 1984 a conference took place in Tripoli of some well-known international terrorists. Among them were Ahmed Jibril of the PFLP General Command, a former Syrian Army demolitions expert trained in the Soviet Union, and Fusako Shigenobu, a notorious member of the Japanese Red Army, who had just flown in from Damascus. That same week Louis Farrakhan, who has predicted a cataclysmic race war in the United States, was also in Tripoli conferring with Qaddafi. Again, little of this appeared in the Western press.

Dealing effectively with state-sponsored terrorism from Libya and such countries as Syria, Iran, South Yemen, Cuba, Nicaragua, and North Korea would be a good beginning for the free world's war with international terrorism. But it would not go to the heart of our problem. This remains our reluctance to recognize that our self-avowed enemy, the Soviet Union, considers itself in a permanent, albeit indirect, state of war with us. Terrorism is an important part of the Soviet arsenal. The media of the democratic world must face up to this reality.

Deny Them Publicity

JOHN O'SULLIVAN

A TERRORIST is a criminal who seeks publicity. This sets him far apart from what British officials in Northern Ireland have taken to calling the ODC, or Ordinary Decent Criminal, who understandably shuns the limelight. Indeed, it is an understatement to say that terrorists seek publicity. They *require* publicity. It is their lifeblood. If the media were not there to report terrorist acts and to explain their political and social significance (the motives inspiring them and so forth), terrorism as such would cease to exist. Each terrorist act would then be seen merely as an isolated criminal event. It would not be interpreted as an integral part of a pattern of political violence, the likely prelude to other bombings and shootings, something to be seriously discussed by politicians, bureaucrats, and television sociologists.

The media find terrorism a sensational news story and are therefore inclined at first to overreport it, to write admiringly of the terrorists' "daring," even while morally condemning them, and to exaggerate their significance. The media exploit terrorism as a good story, but they could do without it. If it were not there, however, other equally newsworthy topics would be at hand—wars, demonstrations, elections, congressional battles, the marriages of pop stars, and, of course, ordinary decent crime.

What benefits does the terrorist seek from media publicity? In what way does he hope to make the media his accomplices? There are three types of unwitting media assistance. They help the terrorist spread an atmosphere of fear and anxiety in society, they provide him with an opportunity to argue his case to the wider public, and they bestow an undeserved legitimacy on him.

Let us take the first, the spreading of fear and anxiety through society. This seems to be achieved principally by simple media coverage of the terrorist's act. Such reports naturally arouse public concern; it would be alarming if they did not. In a free society, however, nothing is to be done about this. A regime like that of the Soviet Union can suppress all news of its occasional hijackings, as it does news of airline crashes and major industrial disasters. If events do not become known, they cannot influence public opinion. (Even this argument cannot be pushed too far; if terrorist acts were sufficiently frequent, they would become known through gossip and hearsay even in the most effectively censored society.)

Is panic contrived by terrorists, then, simply the unavoidable price of living in a society with a free press? I do not think so. For it is not the mere succession of terrorist acts which when reported arouses public anxiety. Statistically, these are usually a very trivial threat to the lives and limbs of anyone in particular. Rather, the media heighten tension by reporting not just the terrorists' acts but also their threats of *future* violence, by describing in often lurid colors the campaign of terror that will ensue if the government does not meet terrorist demands, giving the impression that endless violence and upheaval lie ahead.

This spreads panic and anxiety in two ways. First, it directly increases the ordinary citizen's fear that he may fall victim to a bomb in a restaurant or a supermarket. But also, more subtly, it conveys the message that society is in moral chaos, that its laws, rules, standards, and securities no longer provide any protection against random violence. There is an instructive comparison from the world of crime. People are murdered all the time without arousing any public feeling more profound than a prurient curiosity. But when a killer like the Yorkshire Ripper not merely kills people but also mutilates them and then mocks society and the police for their inability to stop him, a genuine fear based on moral uncertainty grips the public. In short, the media can magnify terrorist violence so that its impact on public opinion is disproportionate to the actual physical harm it does.

In these circumstances pressure grows for the government to take action to restore public order. This is more likely to be pressure for repressive measures than for government concessions, an awkward result for the terrorists. To take account of this, philosophers of terrorism produced a theory whereby terror would produce a repressive government, which in turn would alienate the people by its repression, which would at last usher in a revolutionary government to the terrorists' taste. This has turned out to be wishful thinking. Democratic governments in Britain, Italy, and West Germany have been able to reduce or eliminate terrorism without abandoning democratic institutions.

I turn now to the second way in which the media unwittingly assist terrorism: they provide the terrorist with an opportunity to broadcast his views to the wider public. This is an opportunity which he would not generally enjoy if he were to use the conventional channels of democratic politics, because the support he would generate would not warrant that kind of media attention. But the use of terror gives him a platform. The reason is, once again, straightforward journalistic curiosity. Who are these people blowing up restaurants, shooting policemen, hijacking planes? Why are they doing it? What are their aims, intentions, philosophies? And what are their demands? The press assumes that the public is clamoring to know the answers to such questions, and seeks to provide them. The terrorists themselves so arrange their affairs as to make life relatively easy for the media. They arrange press conferences, publish "communiqués" and statements of ultimate aims, and give exclusive interviews. In Northern Ireland, the so-called Republic Movement is divided into a terrorist wing which murders people, the IRA, and a political wing, Sinn Fein, which is available to the media to explain why these murders were regrettable necessities. The PLO has a similar arrangement, complementing its terror apparatus with a full-fledged international press operation.

We can judge the importance which the terrorists attach to the media by the fact that they often force the media to present their case by threatening to kill hostages if the media refuse. In

1975, for instance, the Montaneros terrorists in Buenos Aires released a Mercedes-Benz director after his company had published advertisements in Western newspapers denouncing the "economic imperialism" of multinational corporations in the Third World.

This presents a problem for both press and politicians in a democratic society. It is our natural instinct to publish some incomprehensible verbiage which few will read and by which no one will be influenced, in return for saving lives. We comfort ourselves that on such occasions the terrorists are falling victim to their own delusions about the power of advertising to influence social and political attitudes. If that were so, the only effect of such advertisements would be to swell the revenues of newspapers. But such reasoning ignores the long-term consequences of letting the terrorist be seen to bargain with governments and dictate to the media. Not only does he thereby raise his political status dramatically, he also obtains the "Robin Hood" glamour of having triumphed, however trivially, from a position of relative weakness. And by permitting their own denunciation, governments and media come off as somehow corrupt, certainly impotent. One answer is for governments to announce in advance, as Edward Heath's government did in 1973, that they will not bargain if one of their number is abducted. Such a declaration strengthens their moral authority when they urge private bodies to resist similar blackmail.

It is, however, the concentration by the media on the terrorist's "case" that gives rise to the third, and perhaps most difficult, problem: the unwitting bestowal of respectability upon terrorist groups. Talking about the aims and philosophies of terrorists inevitably conveys the impression that they are a species of politician rather than a species of criminal. We begin to think of the terrorist in relation to economic or foreign policy rather than in relation to kneecapping, amputations, and point-blank murder. Yet it is what the terrorist *does* rather than what he *thinks* (or says he thinks) that makes him a legitimate object of media attention. After all, some people *like* killing and hurting and frightening others. That insight might be a far more reliable guide to the terrorist's "motivation" than some parroted guff about social or political justice and institutionalized violence. It might also be a better guide to his future actions.

Television presents this problem of legitimacy in a particularly acute form, for it conveys a sort of respectability upon the terrorist simply by interviewing him. Television is a leveling and homogenizing medium by its very nature, and the process of interviewing someone, whether he is a terrorist or a foreign diplomat or a government official, is essentially the same process. The producer and interviewer might well go to considerable lengths to show the terrorist in a bad light. No matter how aggressive the questioner is, however, he could hardly be more aggressive than, say, Robin Day interrogating Mrs. Thatcher or Dan Rather grilling Mr. Nixon. Even if the terrorist comes off badly, therefore, he will achieve his aim by being treated as someone whose contribution to public debate is worthy of attention. He becomes by degrees a politician.

Is there some compensating advantage that justifies such interviews? I do not believe there is. The blunt truth is that a terrorist is an advocate of murder and that the advocacy of murder is, or should be, beyond the acceptable boundaries of public discussion. The justification commonly advanced is that "we need to know what these people think." But that is nonsense. To begin with, we invariably know what they think long before they appear on television to tell us. Is anyone unaware of the aims and beliefs of the PLO, or of the IRA, or of the Red Brigades? Secondly, what they say on television is not necessarily what they think (which, as I have argued above, is much more accurately conveyed by what they do). It is sugared propaganda. Finally, even if we needed to know what the terrorist thought and could rely on his honesty, a straightforward report and analysis by the journalist himself would be a more efficient and reliable method of conveying such information without the side effect of conferring legitimate respectability upon murderers.

Thus far we have considered rather general examples of the media's influence in relation to terrorism. But there have also been a number of occasions on which newspaper and television reporting of specific terrorist incidents has actually hampered the authorities. For instance, in the 1977 hijacking of a Lufthansa jet, the terrorists heard over the radio news that the German captain was passing information to the authorities over his flight radio frequency. They subsequently killed him. A similar incident, which fortunately did not have so tragic a result, occurred during the London siege of the Iranian embassy. BBC television viewers suddenly found a television program interrupted by live coverage of the start of the SAS operation to lift the siege. Fortunately, the terrorists were not watching. If they had been, some of the hostages might have perished.

What attitudes in the media contribute to problems I have outlined? One attitude is the exaggeration of the reasonable view that press and government are necessarily antagonistic, the press bent upon exposure and defending the public's right to know, the government insisting upon its executive privacy. Whatever virtue this may have in the ordinary political rough-and-tumble, it is not an appropriate attitude when the authorities are coping with a campaign of murder. Leaks of government plans and ignoring official requests for a news blackout when lives are at stake represent a professional distortion of proper human priorities. Fortunately, this is not always so. In the Martin Schleyer kidnapping, for example, the media observed requests for strict silence on official actions.

Another problematic attitude is what Conor Cruise O'Brien calls "unilateral liberalism," which is as common in the media as it is in the new class. O'Brien describes this as the "kind of liberalism which is sensitive exclusively to threats to liberty seen as emanating from the democratic state itself, and is curiously phlegmatic about threats to liberty from the enemies of that state." It is this attitude that underlies the belief that, in some sense, the terrorists have a right to have their case presented, as if murder were a sort of opinion which the public should respect.

Finally, there is an attitude that requires little elaboration— the pursuit of commercial and professional competition, which allows no self-restraint in covering a dramatic story.

The most important contribution that the media could make to defeating terrorism would be changing such attitudes. Other aspects of media coverage would then change automatically.

The Price of Sympathy

LORD CHALFONT

TERRORISM would be impotent without publicity. It is utterly
dependent on the media to compel and hold public attention.
This is one reason terrorists attack innocent civilians. A soldier
shot in the back in Belfast may merit a few lines in the national
papers, and probably none in the international press; but a restaurant or a supermarket bombed in a city center, with women
and children killed and mutilated, or an airliner hijacked and
subsequently blown up, will get headlines and prime-time treatment. The fact that the deed may cause widespread revulsion
and outrage is not only of no concern to the terrorist; it actually
serves his purpose. The aim of terrorism, as Lenin said, is to
terrorize, and the more brutal and apparently senseless the attack, the better for the terrorists.

Terrorism can be fought effectively only if we establish a sympathetic and supportive climate of public opinion. One of the
principal instruments in achieving this ought to be the free press
and communications media of the West. Yet our newspapers,
radio, and television have probably done more than the terrorist
organizations themselves to make terrorist violence glamorous
and successful.

Terrorists have often shown great sophistication in manipu-
lating the media. An illuminating case is that of the Symbionese
Liberation Army, which emerged from nowhere when it kidnapped Patty Hearst. For months the SLA received unprece-

dented exposure on American television and in the press; its tape recordings were broadcast endlessly; an enormous operation, involving a great number of police and FBI agents, was mounted to search for its members. Yet this organization never consisted of more than a dozen people, and its exploits, apart from the sensational abduction of Miss Hearst, were no more than small-time criminal operations. Their prominence was due, almost entirely, to media coverage.

It must be admitted, of course, that violence makes good copy. A machine-gun attack on a bank makes exciting reading, and in a free press journalists report and editors print what they believe to be exciting for their readers. Yet the matter cannot be allowed to rest there, because it can be argued that in this particular context freedom of the press is being abused, or at least manipulated, cynically and irresponsibly.

There are of course a number of journalists who actively sympathize with the criminal activities of terrorist movements, especially the minority that believes in the destruction of capitalist societies. Others assist less consciously in the promotion of terrorism by accepting terrorist organizations at face value and by adopting their terminology. For example, IRA murders in Northern Ireland are reported as "executions" and the brutal torture of soldiers and civilians as "trials" or "interrogations."

Some journalists adopt a false intellectual objectivity that regards the terrorist and the policeman as two sides of a morally symmetrical conflict. It is possible to find in publications of otherwise impeccable respectability the phrase "state violence" used to describe military or police action against terrorists. Some journalists apparently find it difficult to distinguish between an attack by a violent minority on the institutions of a democratic state and the right of that state to defend itself. This is demonstrated by the frequent television appearances of terrorists and their spokesmen, who are allowed to disseminate violent propaganda with the same freedom as candidates for Parliament.

It is not surprising, therefore, that many reasonable persons, especially young people, have failed to understand the nature of terrorism. In such a climate of opinion, governments find it difficult to act decisively against terrorists. But the balance between freedom and order must be subjected to constant re-appraisal. The press of the free world should re-examine its attitudes to subversion and international terrorism. It should realize that its own freedom is conditional upon the larger freedom of the society of which it is a part; when the larger freedom is destroyed, its own will disappear with it. This is not to suggest that news of terrorist activities should be suppressed, but that it should be reported coldly and factually, deprived of its excitement and glamour. Gunmen and bombers should not be interviewed respectfully, as though they were delivering an address on the state of the nation; and those journalists who seek a fallacious moral symmetry should remember that their freedom to report and comment is always the first casualty of terrorism's success.

The only alternative to self-regulation is interference by the state. This suggestion evokes cries of outrage from the newspaper offices and television studios. Yet in wartime, the free nations of the world willingly accept a degree of press censorship to prevent damage to national security. Unless newspaper editors, and those who control our radio and television programs, recognize their responsibility and act accordingly, they might well find themselves facing pressure for some kind of legislative regulation over the reporting of terrorism and the interviewing of terrorists.

When confronted with criticism about interviews with terrorists, the classic reply from the media is that "the public has a right to know" and that the duty of a journalist is to report the news. But this "right to know" surely does not mean that the media should offer an unlimited platform for the terrorist to state his "case." Again, this confusion on the part of many journalists stems from a belief that there is some position of neutrality, or objectivity, as between the terrorist and the establishment which he is seeking to destroy; and that it is the duty of the journalist to occupy this position, dispensing judgment with magisterial authority.

But there is no such position of objectivity, any more than there is, to adapt a phrase of Winston Churchill's, any position of neutrality between the arsonist and the fire brigade. Terrorism is not unlike most other forms of warfare in which the journalist must take sides. He must decide whether a news item, or even a scoop, is more important than defeating a menace to the fabric of free society. For being a journalist does *not* absolve a citizen from the need to "decide that this lot is good, or bad." If there are those in the press who are prepared to sanction terrorist violence as the only way of removing a real or imagined grievance, they should also face up to the certainty that in a society ruled by brute force theirs will be the first freedom to disappear. Unhappily, it will not be the last.

VI

THE LEGAL FOUNDATIONS FOR
THE WAR AGAINST TERRORISM

THE QUESTION of the legal foundations for the struggle against terrorism is not merely a matter of formalism. This is so not only because democracies are based on the rule of law but equally because they are *moral* societies. That is, they operate, or seek to operate, within the constraints of morality. And legality, while not identical to morality, provides a useful approximation to it, just as domestic law approximates, however imperfectly, a society's ideas of justice.

In seeking to fight international terrorism, democracies are particularly anxious to ensure that their responses are lawful and just. Lawful means compliance with the doctrines of international law and the rules of war, as these have been codified over the years. Yet most of this doctrine was formulated in the nineteenth century and the first half of the twentieth. Its most recent major instruments, the United Nations Charter and the Geneva Conventions, were written shortly after World War II, well before international terrorism achieved its present prominence. Is this body of law, designed for an earlier era, capable of addressing a new type of war, terrorism?

Several questions arise: Can governments pursue terrorists to their countries of origin or support? How much force can they apply? Against whom? What about the prospect of killing or injuring innocent people? And what about the question of diplomatic immunity when the terrorists are either sheltered by a foreign embassy or, indeed, *are* the operatives of a foreign government?

These questions stem in part from the tension between the right of sovereignty and the right of self-defense. The democracies have often been hampered in defending themselves against *international* terrorism, which invariably involves the support of states, by an absolutist definition of sovereignty; the effect has been to shelter precisely those regimes with least regard for the sovereignty of others. Not by chance, the terrorist states are quick to invoke the protection of international conventions when any action is contemplated or carried out against them.

How to resolve this conflict? What rights *do* the targets of terrorism have? Imperfect as it is, international law (and the literature of ethics accompanying it) does provide answers. This body of thought, as Michael Walzer points out, makes a clear distinction between the *ends* and the *means* of war. It further distinguishes between just (or lawful) and unjust (or unlawful) ends, and between just and unjust means. In the case of terrorist war, the point of departure is the choice of means. Initiating a systematic and deliberate attack on non-combatants has been for centuries recognized as immoral and unjust. It has been explicitly prohibited by international law, and relegated to the status of a war crime. One does not need to be a lawyer to know the difference between the killing of soldiers and the deliberate slaughter of women and children. Terrorism thus violates the most basic precept of law and common morality.

Why, then, is there a question at all about its legitimacy? This arises from a confusion about the *ends* of terrorists. It is argued that terrorism, however unsavory, is nevertheless in the right when it is pursued for just ends. But *nothing* justifies terrorism, whatever the professed cause. In practice there *is* a definite relationship between the ends of terrorists and the means they choose. Far from fulfilling their promise of liberation, terrorists that have come to power have an unbroken record of internal oppression and external aggression. Terrorism conducted by such groups or states is merely one more instrument of such aggression against which the attacked countries, under both international law and common sense, have every legal and moral right to defend themselves.

The Legality of State Response to Acts of Terrorism

YEHUDA Z. BLUM

THE QUESTION of state response to terrorism touches upon essential problems of contemporary international law, such as the concepts of the non-use of force, aggression, reprisals, and self-defense.

I want to examine these matters in relation to *international* terrorism, since authentically indigenous terrorism seems to be increasingly the exception rather than the rule. The traditional civil-war concept does not necessarily apply, because many so-called civil wars are frequently not genuine civil wars.

As terrorism is often carried out with the encouragement or acquiescence of a sanctuary state, it is unrealistic to expect that state to cooperate with the victim in fighting terrorism. The attacked state is likely to have to seek out the terrorists itself. It might have to send military forces across international boundaries or within armistice lines and, in doing so, encounter criticism. There is, after all, a widely held belief that under the United Nations Charter a state may not resort to the use of force internationally except for self-defense.

Practice, of course, does not necessarily conform to this belief. The French bombardment of Sakiet-Sidi-Youssef in 1958, the British attack on Harib in the Yemen in 1964, the American action in the Gulf of Tonkin in 1965, and the many incidents along the Sino-Soviet border over recent decades show that all the permanent members of the United Nations Security Council have on occasion used force in circumstances which are hard to characterize as self-defense, unless Article 51 of the Charter is stretched beyond its commonly accepted interpretation. Nor have lesser powers behaved differently. In fact, the use of force in circumstances beyond the narrow definition of self-defense has become so widespread that it severely challenges the validity of the prohibition on reprisals. The dominant view continues to regard force as impermissible, and recognizes self-defense as the only exception to the general prohibition on the use of force contained in Article 2(4) of the UN Charter. But in recent years there is a growing conviction that military reprisals may be permissible under exceptional circumstances.

What, then, is the distinction between permissible self-defense and impermissible reprisals? Is it reprisal or self-defense when a state's armed forces attack a marauding group which has just completed its mission and has returned across the border? Does it matter if that group is likely to strike again as soon as it eludes the pursuing force? Such questions show how difficult it is to distinguish clearly between reprisals and self-defense.

The UN Charter prohibits the use of force (Article 2[4]) while obliging states to settle their disputes by peaceful means (Article 2[3]). These two Charter principles cannot be divorced from each other; they are, in fact, two sides of the same coin. A state unwilling to settle peacefully its disputes with another state and preferring to harass it with terrorist raids and military incursions can scarcely be entitled to invoke the principle of the non-use of force in international relations. That theory and practice have placed a much greater emphasis on Article 2(4) than on Article 2(3) compounds the problem. For any approach that undermines the intricate connection between these two Charter principles can only benefit the international lawbreaker.

Armed reprisals have been repeatedly condemned by states and international organizations as a violation of international law. Let us examine, therefore, the alternative recourse, namely, self-defense. Admittedly, shifting emphasis from reprisals to self-defense may be considered by some as an exercise in semantics, which it probably is; yet given the indisputable potency of language symbols, there is no reason to disregard this aspect of international law.

To determine if a military response by the attacked state against the sanctuary state may be termed self-defense, we must first define the legal nature of the terrorist acts and the responsibility of the sanctuary state. A convenient point of departure is the 1951 Draft Code of Offenses Against the Peace and Security of Mankind, prepared by the International Law Commission.

Using a principle established at the Nuremberg trials, the draft code defines as an international crime "the organization, or the encouragement . . . by the authorities of a State, of armed bands within its territory or any other territory for incursions into the territory of another State, or the toleration of the organization of such bands in its own territory, or the toleration of the use by such armed bands of its territory as a base of operations or as a point of departure for incursions into the territory of another State, as well as direct participation in or support of such incursions" (Article 2[4] as revised in 1954).

Such behavior is often regarded as "indirect aggression." Some, however, believe that to give military aid such as weapons, training, and haven should be called aggression, pure and simple.

On December 14, 1974, the UN General Assembly adopted a deliberately narrower definition of aggression. Referring to the dispatch of armed bands, it called aggression, among other things, "the sending by or on behalf of a State of armed bands, groups, irregulars or mercenaries, which carry out acts of armed force against another State of *such gravity as to amount to the acts listed above*." This definition was the result of fierce opposition from Arab and some African states to the broader definition of aggression. They feared that any broader wording would have made them internationally accountable for the acts of terrorism originating from their territories. But the acts of aggression which were listed in the definition are not exhaustive. Other forms of aggression may still be regarded as such, despite their absence from the definition.

Some have argued that, in speaking of "armed attack," Article 51 of the Charter refers only to *direct* attacks by states. But terrorist actions are regarded at most as *indirect* attacks. Ironically, in 1958 the Lebanese UN representative categorically rejected this argument. During a period when his country was the victim of externally stimulated terrorism, the Lebanese delegate told the Security Council: "Article 51 of the Charter speaks not of direct armed attack but of armed attack pure and simple. Article 51 is thus intended to cover all cases of attack, whether direct or indirect, provided it is an armed attack."

The main question is, of course, whether acts of terrorism should be considered as "armed attack" under Article 51. Much depends on whether one is inclined to give a narrow or a broad interpretation of the words "if an armed attack occurs." Here the quantitative element is of great significance. The extent of terrorist activity is relevant in assessing the plea of self-defense. Obviously, one would have to treat an isolated terrorist act differently from an act of terrorism which is but one link in a long chain of such acts, particularly when it is obvious that so many such acts could not have been carried out without the encouragement, knowledge, or acquiescence of another state.

Each of the acts of terrorism, when viewed separately, might not qualify as an "armed attack," but the totality of such acts may reveal such a pattern. This has been called *Nadelstichtaktik* ("tactics of the needle prick") by German international lawyers. This approach holds that while each needle prick in itself may not amount to a serious and intolerable injury to the victim, the overall effect of many needle pricks may be serious and intolerable.

There is another important point here. Under the narrow interpretation of Article 51, the right of self-defense may be exercised "if an armed attack occurs," i.e., while an armed attack is actually taking place, but neither before nor after it. Since terrorist organizations always use hit-and-run tactics, it is often impossible to foil their attacks while they are occurring. The attacked state has to respond afterward. But under the needle-prick approach, such military action may be considered a legitimate response in anticipation of the next terrorist attack.

The narrow interpretation of Article 51 is not only unrealistic in this era of intercontinental ballistic missiles but also incompatible with the traditional concept of the right of self-defense.

What about the question of proportionality? Obviously, the use of force in self-defense has to be proportional to the terrorist actions to which it responds or which it anticipates. If each of the needle pricks to which the attacked state is subjected is viewed in isolation, then a massive response may naturally seem excessive and disproportionate. If, however, one views such response in the broader context of violence to which the victim has been subjected, one may reach an entirely different conclusion.

Proportionality is difficult to judge because it is often impossible for a government to single out and strike at the terrorists within the sanctuary state without at the same time hitting other individuals not directly involved in the terrorists' activities. Terrorists, as we know, often seek cover among the general population. The inevitable outcome is that any attack on terrorist headquarters or installations also endangers people other than the terrorists themselves. But from the legal point of view, an attacked state is entitled to regard the sanctuary state itself as the aggressor, whether or not that state has been unwilling, or unable, to curb terrorist activities from its territory.

Should states be restricted in acting against sanctuary states if the latter seem unable to curb terrorist activity? Even if we could determine whether a sanctuary state was willing, but unable, to suppress the terrorists operating from its territory, the distinction would still be irrelevant, since sovereignty is made up of rights and corresponding obligations.

What about terrorist activities justified by invoking the right of self-determination? It has become fashionable in recent years to deny the right of self-defense to states responding to terrorists asserting such a cause, particularly when it is recognized by states or international organizations. It is claimed that passages in various United Nations resolutions support this contention. But nothing in the UN Charter justifies such claims. The United Nations was founded on the principle of the sovereign equality of all its members. The right of self-defense is recognized by it as an inherent right, one which antedates the Charter and exists independently of it. Any attempt to deprive a state of this right would be in clear violation of the Charter principle of equality of states. The concept of self-determination is permanently subordinated to the dominant purpose of the United Nations, the maintenance of international peace and security. Thus no state or group may legitimately breach the peace, whatever the alleged purpose.

London's Libyan Embassy Shootout: A Case of International Terrorism

ARTHUR J. GOLDBERG

STATE-SUPPORTED TERRORISM calls into question some long held and widely shared assumptions about the degree of immunity which should be accorded to diplomats, diplomatic missions, and diplomatic bags. When the Libyan terrorists murdered British Police Constable Yvonne Fletcher and successfully claimed immunity under the Vienna Convention on Diplomatic Relations, this raised the question whether civilized nations can protect themselves, with due compliance with the rule of law, against individuals and governments which have utter contempt for law, treaties, conventions, and the norms of civilized conduct.

The two gunmen in the Libyan "People's Bureau" in London opened fire on a crowd of anti-Qaddafi demonstrators. Those demonstrators were conducting a peaceful legal protest on a sidewalk adjacent to the People's Bureau. In plain view, the gunmen inside fired from an open window, riddling the demonstrators with automatic gunfire, killing Constable Fletcher, and wounding eleven others. The unarmed policewoman was shot in the back. She was facing the demonstrators to keep them orderly and to provide security for the Libyans. Ten days after this barbaric incident, the British government provided the killers, along with their murder weapons, with safe passage out of the country.

On the day that British police escorted the murderers to

Heathrow Airport, Constable Fletcher was buried. Truly it was a day of infamy. At her funeral, the Home Secretary, Mr. Leon Brittan, stated that the British police were prevented under the terms of the Vienna Convention on Diplomatic Relations from storming the People's Bureau and apprehending the killers. Mr. Brittan claimed Her Majesty's Government could not act because the murderers, the premises of the People's Bureau, and the bags within which the lethal weapons were concealed were all immune according to the convention. This view was reaffirmed in the debate on this issue in the House of Commons by Prime Minister Thatcher and the Foreign Secretary.

As Julian Amery has pointed out, however, constitutions, statutes, and treaties must be construed. The Vienna Convention, like all such great documents, must be sensibly interpreted. In this age of state-sponsored terrorism, the Vienna Convention need not and should not be allowed to be a suicide pact for civilized countries. Treaties, by established legal doctrine, must be read in their entirety, with some provisions necessarily modified by others. Nothing could be more foolish than to accept a simpleminded, literal reading of selected articles of the convention. The privileges and immunities granted by the convention are rights formulated in words. The reality behind those words must not be lost.

The purpose of the Vienna Convention was to grant immunity only to bona fide diplomatic agents, to bona fide embassies, and to bona fide diplomatic bags, not to terrorists masquerading as diplomats. The two Libyan killers, the People's Bureau that housed them, and the pouches that contained their weapons were not afforded immunity by the treaty.

Libya's London embassy was seized some time before by Qaddafi's self-styled revolutionary student adherents. The accredited Libyan diplomats in London, not removed from their posts, were forced to discharge their diplomatic functions under the direction of a non-diplomatic revolutionary committee designated as a "People's Bureau." Under Article 4, Section 1, of the Vienna Convention, the host country has the right before accepting and accrediting a diplomat to review his nomination and, if it is deemed unacceptable, to refuse accreditation. But press accounts report that the killers' names were never submitted to the British government as diplomatic agents. If this is true, the British government was denied the right guaranteed by the Vienna Convention to refuse their acceptance and deny their accreditation. From the evidence available, the killers were not accepted as diplomats.

The British police, after a superficial interview with the Libyans shortly before they departed, issued a statement saying they were diplomats. How the police arrived at this conclusion is not clear. Diplomatic passports are not conclusive evidence. For example, because of my long government service, I myself have been issued a diplomatic passport by the State Department as a courtesy. I am certainly not, however, a diplomatic agent as defined by the Vienna Convention.

Indeed, it appears that the Libyan chargé d'affaires in London who conducted Libya's legitimate diplomatic business with the British government was not a revolutionary but a professional diplomat. This person was accepted and accredited by the British Foreign Office. Though acceptance by the head of state of the receiving country is the more common procedure, acceptance of a "chargé" by the Foreign Office is permitted in some cases by the convention. Although a professional diplomat, the chargé nonetheless performed his functions under the direction of the revolutionary committee.

Even if the British government had accepted the terrorists as diplomatic representatives, their conduct as terrorists, under any evolving concept of international law, constitutes a forfeiture of their right to be recognized as bona fide diplomatic agents. And even if they were diplomatic agents, they were not free from arrest. Diplomats have frequently been arrested. After arrest, they must plead diplomatic immunity, and if entitled to it and supported by proof under the Vienna Convention, they must be released. In this instance, however, the British made no arrests. The British police merely conducted a brief interview before the killers left for Libya, apparently in an attempt to pacify the British public by allowing the government to say that the Libyans were at least questioned by the British police.

But there was also the issue of the embassy's inviolability, as the Home Secretary pointed out. He claimed that under the Vienna Convention the police had no right to storm the People's Bureau, capture the killers, and confiscate their weapons. I disagree. Qaddafi's London People's Bureau can scarcely qualify as a bona fide embassy whose premises are inviolable under the Vienna Convention. In charge of the building, as I have noted, was a committee of non-diplomats for whom accredited diplomats were obliged to work. Genuine embassies do not function in this manner.

Furthermore, there is reliable evidence that the People's Bureau harbored teams sent to assassinate Libyan dissidents. Terrorist murder factories are not embassies, and therefore do not come within the scope of the Vienna Convention. That treaty is designed to grant immunity to a real embassy devoted to diplomatic relations. Article 41, Section 3, of the convention states that the "premises of the mission must not be used in any manner incompatible with the functions of the mission as laid down in the . . . Convention or by other rules of international law . . ." Harboring hit squads clearly does not come within the protection of that provision. The People's Bureau in London, therefore, was not a bona fide embassy. It was subject under established rules of international law to search and seizure by the British police after the brutal murder of Constable Fletcher and the wounding of peaceful demonstrators on the sidewalk.

The Home Secretary claimed that the Libyans' diplomatic bags could not be searched, despite official statements that the murder weapons were probably brought into the country in these bags and spirited out in the same way. While Article 27, Section 2, of the convention states that diplomatic bags are inviolable, another related provision, Section 4, states that a diplomatic bag "must contain only diplomatic documents or articles intended for official use." Murder weapons hardly meet that requirement. The various provisions of the convention are obviously intended to be read together under settled rules of treaty interpretation. It is strange that in the case of the incident involving the Nigerian exile Dikko the British government felt free, justifiably in my opinion, to open a crate labeled diplomatic baggage, in contrast to its inhibition to open the Libyan bag containing the murder weapon.

There is substantial evidence that diplomatic bags are indeed being abused, by some countries besides Libya, to transfer such weapons. What if they were used to carry conventional or nuclear bombs? An excessively liberal interpretation of the convention's terms means we could all go up in smoke.

When the Libyan killers struck, the British government could have, within the terms of the convention, raided the People's Bureau, arrested the murderers, and seized the material evidence. Why, then, did officials at the highest levels of the British government consistently state that they could not bring the killers to justice because of the Vienna Convention? There are at least two possible reasons.

First, the British government was properly concerned about the safety of the British mission in Libya and that of the eight thousand Britons who were employed in that country.

I believe that this fear was unfounded. The United States broke off relations with Libya some time ago. Despite this, over two thousand Americans continued to reside and work in Libya. They did not appear to be at risk, nor did the American diplomats who remained in Tripoli in the Special Interest sections of a friendly government embassy. Qaddafi clearly values the technological help these Americans provide; this is also true of the British citizens in Libya. But even if Qaddafi's response to a British raid on the London People's Bureau had been violent, the British government should not have acted as it did. Qaddafi's commitment to terrorism is known to all; British citizens and workers who choose to remain in Libya for commercial reasons knowingly put themselves at risk.

Second, the conclusion seems almost inescapable that rather than letting the killers go in compliance with the provisions of diplomatic immunity, the British government was, in fact, protecting its commercial interests in Libya. This is an unacceptable justification.

The only step Britain took in response to this horrible crime was to sever diplomatic relations with Libya. This was simply a slap on the wrist. Business as usual continued between the two countries. Some British diplomats remained in Libya, housed in a Special Interest section in a friendly nation's embassy. A number of Libyans remained in London in a similar arrangement.

Surely a different response was called for. Libya has embassies and consulates all over the world, probably all under the control of cadres like those who took over the People's Bureau in London. As head of state, after all, Qaddafi has shown himself to be one of the world's foremost proponents of international terrorism, supporting terrorists with vast supplies of Soviet arms. After the expulsion of the Libyan terrorists from Britain, he declared that he was dispatching more hit squads abroad and, on television, gave the killers of Constable Fletcher a hero's welcome.

The issue, then, is how civilized nations can combat this threat to their survival, their freedom, and the rule of law. The British government's weak response to Libyan terrorism was the worst reaction possible to state-supported terrorism. Terrorist blackmail must never be countenanced.

Probably to allay the justifiable outrage of the British public, the government said it would seek amendments to the Vienna Convention to take account of the abuse of diplomatic credentials and privileges by countries which support terrorism. The practical problems involved in amending the convention dictate against such an approach; the Soviet Union, its allies, the Arab states, and many neutral and non-aligned countries will not agree to any amendments. Certainly Libya and other terrorist states will not endorse amendments.

The British government has been correctly criticized for relying on the Vienna Convention to excuse its failure to act against the murderers. The British approach blurs the distinction between terrorists and accredited diplomats. That confusion poses a great danger. When democratic governments tell their citizens that there is no difference between the two, they discourage respect for the rule of law and bona fide diplomatic immunity. The price Britain and other civilized countries pay when they choose to submit to terrorist blackmail, under the subterfuge of spurious diplomatic immunity, encourages rather than deters

terrorism. For terrorism, unless checked, breeds further terrorism.

Terrorism can best be fought by the united actions of the
democracies. Without a coordinated and effective international
anti-terrorist program, no country can be faulted for attempting
to treat this problem on its own as long as it does not resort to
extra-legal measures. It has been suggested that the way to fight
terrorism by democratic countries is by extra-legal means. I
emphatically disagree. Although we cannot change terrorists,
they must not be allowed to change us. Our war against terrorism
must be waged to preserve democratic values and adherence to
the rule of law, and must not erode these foundations of our
society. The arsenal of legal weapons under international law
available to democracies is formidable enough to curb terrorism,
if sufficient resolve and resources are dedicated to this task.

In the Libyan shootout, the British government and most of
the British political establishment disregarded Churchill's maxim
that in a national crisis the first mandate is Resolution. Britain,
admirable in so many respects, lacked resolve in this matter.
Regrettably, it was not her "finest hour."

Overcoming Denial

EUGENE ROSTOW

WE ALL understand what is happening in the world. But we resist confronting our knowledge, as our fathers resisted confronting the truth about Hitler fifty years ago. This resistance is not primarily derived from ignorance, cowardice, stupidity, or even from the defects of our educational system. It derives from a deeper source, the psychological mechanism of denial. Denial is a powerful and indispensable factor in our daily lives, permitting us to function without undue anxiety. But denial can also do great harm if it keeps us from recognizing and thwarting real dangers to our survival.

Acting sensibly in good time is the essence of the problem facing Western civilization. What can we do about state-sponsored terrorism? We must first recognize that it is a form of aggression. Aggression is the most serious of all violations of international law, a profound threat to the state system on whose stability and viability peace depends.

The greatest danger confronting humanity today is not nuclear weapons, pollution, exhaustion of natural resources, or the population explosion, but the state of anarchy which is rapidly spreading as the practice of aggression spreads. Dozens of nations are consumed in the flames of insensate war, and the number will increase unless aggression is brought under control.

Terrorism is perhaps the most pernicious form of aggression. State-sponsored terrorism is war, an act of state policy and not merely of individuals or criminal groups. We should recognize that under international law it is an armed attack, in peace or in war, for which the perpetrators of terrorism, their collaborators, and their host states are absolutely liable. Terrorism will not be extirpated until we create a realistic system of collective self-defense against state-sponsored aggression in all its forms.

It is futile to imagine that the provisions of the United Nations Charter against aggression, and thus against terrorism, can be effectively restored and upheld through the United Nations itself. Such action must be pursued by regional coalitions organized for collective self-defense, with the United States as an indispensable member.

Such arrangements existed and functioned reasonably well from the end of World War II to the 1970s. These were greatly weakened by the tragedy of Vietnam. Although still the formal basis of Western policy, the system of regional defense lacks the confidence, energy, and support of public understanding which sustained the resistance to aggression in Berlin, Iran, Greece, and Korea. Within a reinvigorated regional defense system, terrorism, at least the state-supported variety, would be relatively easy to confront. Without it, all our efforts will fail.

Our strategy against terrorism must move beyond the passive to the active and the preemptive, as the Israelis did against the PLO in Lebanon in 1982. Some have argued that this action was against international law, although defensible nonetheless. But existing international law does not require the victim of aggression to respond only within his own frontiers. Where necessary, the victim may use whatever force is required in time of peace to eliminate the source of aggression against him. This principle is supported by the text and history of Article 51 of the Charter, which provides that nothing in the Charter qualifies the inherent right of self-defense, and by a multitude of precedents in international law which define the historical scope of that inherent right.

Article 51 does not require the victim of a forceful breach of international law to obtain the permission of the Security Council before acting in self-defense. He may act on his own perception of threat. Nor is there any need under Article 51 to wait before defending one's sovereignty until it is too late to do so. President Kennedy's handling of the Cuban missile crisis of 1962 is a perfect example of preemptive self-defense under Article 51.

Israel, too, had an altogether legal right to enter Lebanon to eliminate the source, not only of attacks against Israel itself, but of attacks against Israeli interests throughout the world. Lebanon had a categorical legal obligation to prevent its territory from being used for such purposes. An instructive parallel is the obligation Britain acknowledged in the nineteenth century when it paid heavy damages to the United States for failing to prevent the escape of the Confederate cruiser *Alabama* from a British port during the Civil War. Since Lebanon was incapable of putting down the PLO, Israel had a right to enter Lebanese territory to do what the Lebanese should have done themselves.

Presidents Wilson and Monroe, and many other heads of government, took comparable action to address breaches of international law by other states for which no lesser remedy was available. We must curb our puritanical tendency to blame ourselves for calamities and to doubt our right to resort to vigorous and perfectly legal self-defense.

For now, we can and should protect our interests within the ample framework of the rule of law. We should work to restore its integrity by insisting on reciprocal respect for its norms. The great regional coalitions of nations committed to peace throughout the world have more than enough power to accomplish this goal, if they see things as they are and liberate themselves from the paralyzing influence of denial. They must turn again to their faith as the reservoir from which courage will flow. They must begin to act effectively and with conviction. They must take to heart the lessons of the Bay of Pigs and the Western failure in Lebanon, and do better next time. Above all, they should not deceive themselves by pretending that these setbacks did not happen. They can be sure that both our friends and our adversaries know better.

Constitutional Power and the Defense of Free Government

The Case of Abraham Lincoln

WALTER BERNS

TERRORISM poses basic questions about our capacity to do what is necessary to defend the Constitution and the liberal democracy established under it; by our capacity I mean both the constitutional powers available to us and our willingness to use them.

It is sometimes said by those who argue that the Constitution is out of date that the Founders wrote for a time of muskets and sailing ships and that they could not have anticipated the powers needed to cope with modern conflicts. The world has certainly changed; the world of international politics has, in some respects, changed with it, so much so that we may find it difficult to appreciate the problems our ancestors faced in the eighteenth century. Our diplomats of that time were less likely to be assassinated, but then again, they were more likely to ignore their instructions. In 1791 our first Secretary of State, Thomas Jefferson, complained to William Carmichael, the American minister in Madrid, that he hadn't heard from him in almost two years.

It was a slower world then, but as our Founders saw it, already a world filled with dangers that had to be faced and conquered. And the government they created was designed to do this. As Madison said in a letter to Jefferson: "It is a melancholy reflection that liberty should be equally exposed to danger whether the government have too much or too little power."

But how much power is too much? Contrary to what is usually thought today, the Constitution does not answer that question. Too much power is beyond what is necessary, and it is not given to writers of constitutions to foresee what may be necessary. The *ends* (or purposes) of government are foreseeable and capable of being stated explicitly—a more perfect union, justice, domestic tranquillity, the common defense—but the *means* of promoting those ends (for example, the common defense) cannot be foreseen. As Madison and Hamilton said in *The Federalist Papers*, the means are surely authorized, but only implicitly:

> Wherever a general power to do a thing is given, every particular power necessary for doing it is included . . .
>
> [The powers needed for the common defense] ought to exist without limitation, *because it is impossible to foresee or to define the extent and variety of national exigencies, and the correspondent extent and variety of the means which may be necessary to satisfy them.* The circumstances that endanger the safety of nations are infinite, and for this reason no constitutional shackles can wisely be imposed on the power to which the care of it is committed.
>
> . . . As I know nothing to exempt this portion of the globe from the common calamities that have befallen other parts of it, I acknowledge my aversion to every project that is calculated to disarm the government of a single weapon, which in any possible contingency might be usefully employed for the general defense and security.

The Founders had had experience enough of governments with too little power: a commander in chief during the Revolution wholly dependent on the Continental Congress, state constitutions that imposed every conceivable restraint on the executive in order to reduce him to a position of complete subordination to the legislature, and the Articles of Confederation, the first constitution of the United States, which provided for no executive whatever. Nothing is clearer in the debates of the Constitutional Convention of 1787 than the Founders' intention to avoid these particular mistakes.

The body of the Constitution begins by defining the legislative power, which is to be expected in a document so strongly influenced by the political philosophy of John Locke. The legislative power comes first because, according to Locke, the body politic comes into existence only when men, who are by nature subject to no authority, agree to leave the state of nature by surrendering their natural liberties to civil society. The legislative, Locke says, is the "supreme power." This is the origin of the modern doctrine of the rule of law and the supremacy of law, and the Founders recognized that supremacy by giving the lawmaking branch priority of place. They proceeded, however, to establish an executive whose powers, unlike in a parliamentary system, come not from the legislature but from the people.

By making the executive independent, the Founders acknowledged that, however desirable in principle, in practice not all things that government may have to do to advance the public good can be done by law or formulated in law. I hesitate to say this when I lack the space to say it properly, but under our written Constitution, law is not supreme. Above the law, and the lawmaking body, are the people of the United States, whose will is expressed in the written Constitution. The supremacy of the people over the law is apparent in the first sentence of Article I: "All legislative powers herein granted," thereby indicating that certain legislative powers are not granted. But compare this with the first sentence of Article II: "The executive power shall be vested in a President of the United States of America." There is no suggestion here that any part of the executive power is being withheld. And if John Locke was their guide here, as he was elsewhere, the executive power includes the prerogative, "the power to act according to discretion for the public good, without the prescription of law and sometimes even against it." How great those powers are was demonstrated by Lincoln, in my judgment the greatest of American Presidents.

Lincoln fought a war that was never declared; without congressional authorization, he called for volunteers to fight that war; he established a naval blockade of ports from Texas to Virginia; he suspended the privilege of the writ of habeas corpus; he put enemy sympathizers in army jails without trial and ignored a demand of the Chief Justice to free them; most important, he used his power as commander in chief to free the slaves, something not even Congress was authorized to do. To those who complained that someone sworn "to take care that the laws be faithfully executed" must not violate them, Lincoln pointed out that none of the laws were being "faithfully executed" in nearly one-third of the states. He asked: "Are all the laws but one to go unexecuted; and the government itself go to pieces, lest that one be violated?"

The gentlest of men when the world permitted him to be gentle, he nevertheless authorized the execution, by firing squad, of 267 persons during his presidency. However reluctantly, he did not refrain from punishing those who in exercising what they insisted was their freedom of speech bore some responsibility for the crimes for which the others were being executed. "Must I," he asked, "shoot a simple-minded soldier boy who deserts, while I must not touch a hair of a wily agitator who induces him to desert? . . . I think that, in such a case, to silence the agitator and save the boy is not only constitutional, but a great mercy."

Compare this attitude with a more recent statement on a similar subject. A few years ago, during Senate hearings on a bill prohibiting the disclosure of the names and identities of covert CIA agents, the American Civil Liberties Union said: "A citizen has the right to impair or impede the functions of a government agency, whether it is the Federal Trade Commission or the CIA." Covert agents and the intelligence operations which they engage in are one of the most effective weapons we have against terrorism. The ACLU conceded that we may properly have a Central Intelligence Agency, but insisted that citizens had a constitutional right to disclose the names of CIA agents, even if this undermined the work of the agency.

Beyond the obvious fact that we are not involved in a civil war, or formally in any other kind of war, what distinguishes this case from Lincoln's? Not a lack of constitutional power: the powers are there when they are needed; the Founders saw to that, and they also authorized the President to decide when they were needed. The real difference is a lack of commitment, a sufficiently strong commitment, to the cause of free government. Lincoln spoke of the United States as "the last best hope of earth"; we are not likely to say that, or if we say it, to mean it, or to mean it as Lincoln meant it.

Lincoln spoke powerfully of the blessings of liberty and asked his fellow citizens to make sacrifices for it. When he used that phrase, "the last best hope of earth," he was asking for a great sacrifice. Our politicians are likely to become impassioned only when speaking of the nuclear freeze, or nuclear disarmament, or of Marines dying in Lebanon or Grenada or not dying in Central America. Some of them appear to think that the people prefer welfare to liberty, that Socrates was right when he likened democracy to the deliberations of children empowered to choose between the dietary prescriptions of a physician and those of a pastry chef. We have enough reason to be afraid, but have we not reason enough to avoid being *governed* by our fears? Not as Dr. Seuss and some of his interpreters see it, and their attitudes serve as a metaphor for our predicament.

Dr. Seuss is the author of very popular children's books. They have been best sellers, and he was awarded a Pulitzer Prize. In *The Butter Battle Book* he satirizes the cold war after the fashion of Jonathan Swift. The theme of the book has been described as a satirical parable about the arms race. This time West and East, U.S.A. and U.S.S.R., are cast as the Yooks and the Zooks. They are enemies because the Zooks eat their bread with the down side buttered while the Yooks keep the buttered side up. Some would not argue with the parable, finding accurate Dr. Seuss's portrait of the present world confrontation; which is to say, two old enemies arguing about nothing that matters. If they find fault with Dr. Seuss, it is that he did not provide a happy ending, since what children need from adults is a dose of hope. Not, however, the hope to live as free men and women, but simply the hope to stay alive.

Words precede deeds, and our condition is reflected in our speech and, even more so, in the way we are spoken to. It might even be said that what we are capable of doing depends to a great extent on what we are capable of saying, and what we are capable of saying depends on what we are capable of hearing. The American people began with a Declaration—a statement— of Independence, embodying, as Lincoln was to say, the principle of liberty for all. To safeguard that principle, the Founders pledged to one another their lives, their fortunes, and their sacred honor. Without such a commitment, Lincoln wrote, "we could not, I think, have secured our free government."

These words are part of Lincoln's reflections on a biblical passage, Proverbs 25:11: "A word fitly spoken is like apples of gold in pictures of silver." No American better appreciated the power of words "fitly spoken." In his First Inaugural, he appealed to the Southern states not to secede from the Union with these words: "The mystic chords of memory, stretching from every battlefield and patriot grave to every living heart and hearth-stone, all over this broad land, will yet swell the chorus of the Union, when again touched, as surely they will be, by the better angels of our nature."

But the Civil War came, and what Lincoln later did at Gettysburg was to create new "mystic chords," stretching from a new battlefield, to every living and every future American heart, reminding us of the cause of free government, a cause first expressed in 1776, asking us to dedicate ourselves to the "great task remaining before us," so that the nation, then torn by a civil war, would have a "new birth of freedom." Without such a dedication, government of, by, and for the people, the last best hope of earth, *shall* perish, and the dead who fought for it *shall* have died in vain.

The question now facing America is whether we can still hear those words, and in them the words spoken by the Founders fourscore and seven years earlier, and then can act accordingly, or support actions taken in accordance with them. Or whether, on the contrary, we are willing to be addressed, without being outraged, as Yooks (or Zooks), believing in nothing, standing for nothing, and being prepared to risk nothing at Concord, Gettysburg, or, to bring this paper to a proper close, Entebbe.

Enemies of Mankind

BURTON M. LEISER

TERRORISM is designed to create an atmosphere of despair or fear, and shake the faith of citizens in their government. Terrorists carry out arbitrary and selective murder, kidnapping, assassination, robbery, and bombings. They do so with total indifference to legal and moral norms while claiming special exemption from these norms. They are convinced that the death and suffering of innocent people who have nothing to do with them are justified by the cause they espouse.

One can thus distinguish acts which should be properly classified as terrorism from other types of violence. For example, people who blow up schoolchildren, shoppers, and worshippers, or hijack and blow up civilian airliners, or gun down tourists, moviegoers, and athletes, are clearly terrorists. In contrast, however much one disapproves of the objectives of a revolutionary or subversive organization, it should *not* be called terroristic if it confines its targets to military, police, and government personnel.

We admire the guerrilla fighter tactics practiced in Europe in World War II, not only because they were fighting to rid that continent of Nazism, but also because they directed their attacks against that regime's functionaries. If the partisans had blown up crowded school buses and slaughtered other innocent civilians, our admiration would be misplaced.

Under international law, belligerents do not have the right to use all means at their disposal for attacking the enemy. Even during war, non-combatants may not be deliberately attacked. The murder, mutilation, cruel treatment, and torture of prisoners is forbidden. The taking of hostages is outlawed. Terrorists, however, engage precisely in those acts that have been legally proscribed even in wartime.

It is because of this that the most fitting term for a terrorist is *hostis humani generis*, enemy of mankind. This term was once reserved for pirates, whom Associate Justice Story, echoing Hobbes, called "brutes and beasts of prey." Terrorists should therefore be treated with the utter contempt that any civilized person reserves for those who, given the opportunity, would destroy the very foundation of civilization.

They are a threat to the existence of all free states (as the PLO so clearly showed in Lebanon), a menace to international peace and order, and a threat to civilized society. Every state should regard terrorists as implacable foes who must be eliminated, either by unilateral action or in concert with other like-minded nations. Steadfast refusal to negotiate with them would deprive them of the publicity upon which they thrive. And just as sea piracy was eliminated by a courageous and sustained campaign, every effort should be directed by the democracies to destroy terrorists and their organizations wherever they may be found.

In particular, I propose that the principle of hot pursuit be internationally recognized. Any nation that is attacked in any way by terrorists ought lawfully to be able to pursue these predators wherever they might flee. Any nation that provides aid and comfort to these international outlaws should be subject to appropriate sanctions, including economic sanctions, the severance of communication and transportation lines, the breaking of diplomatic relations, blockade, invasion, and even open warfare. These international outlaws can no longer be permitted to roam free.

An International Convention Against Terrorism

MEIR SHAMGAR

IN 1979, at the Jonathan Institute's first conference, I presented a scheme for international cooperation to combat terrorism. It proposed that the nations of the free world join in an international convention that would provide ways and means for cooperation against this latest form of international lawlessness. It suggested principles under national and international law to deal with the illegality of terrorist offenses, the prosecution or extradition of terrorists, the sharing of intelligence, and preventive measures and sanctions against states that support or consent to terrorism. It called for a conference of governments to draft a convention and lay the ground for legal, political, and strategic cooperation.

Despite the tremendous growth of terrorism since 1979, these proposals have yet to be adopted. It is all the more important to put them forward again in detail. The definition of terrorism that should guide us is that terrorism is "deliberate and systematic murder, maiming, and menacing of the innocent to gain political ends." The murder, maiming, and menacing of human beings is a criminal offense under the legal system of every civilized country, because they are *male in se*.

Despite the consensus on the legal nature of these acts, which do not change their criminal character when committed to further political aims, governments have responded in an unsatisfactory and inconsistent manner on many fronts in the war against terrorism. Such hesitant approaches have led to the weakening of deterrence, a critical element in penology and essential to all punitive measures.

The practice of terrorism has grown immeasurably because of four factors: First, terrorists have achieved political gains from their activity. Second, they have enjoyed the crucial support of states. Third, the terrorists have come to believe that they can effectively spread fear in the general public, weakening the power of resistance of ordinary citizens. Fourth, the terrorists have often perceived a corresponding hesitancy in the response of governments to their challenge.

Further terrorist gains along these lines can best be prevented effectively by an alignment on the international level. This is the only level on which the crucial problem of state support can be addressed. An international convention against terror is important not only because it would promote a concerted effort by nations but also because of the psychological effect it would have. It would shore up the resolve of smaller states which are expected to act on their own but are unable to shoulder the task by themselves. The moral and physical support extended by the co-signatories to such a convention, even the mere *existence* of such co-partners, would eliminate or reduce indecisiveness and encourage appropriate action.

I mentioned hesitancy a moment ago. Hesitancy is not always inappropriate. There are occasions when caution, deliberation, and preparation are warranted. But when inaction is caused by weakness, the results are always bad. The mutual support and combined strength of partners to an international convention may frustrate those relying on their ability to intimidate the weaker nations. And the moral effect would extend beyond the signatories to small states unprepared or unable to join. A convention, then, multiplies deterrence and prevention.

The skepticism that accompanies the signature of an international instrument would not be warranted here. *Pacta sunt servanta* is a maxim which may have never been fully achieved, but that agreements should be honored is a legitimate aim that should be adopted in international relations no less than in legal relations among individuals.

The implementation of the provisions, especially those against state-supported terror, could have a decisive effect on the entire international climate and could considerably reduce terrorist activities. This would produce results diametrically opposed to those expected by the terrorists (namely, frustration and a readiness to capitulate), amounting to a defeat for the terrorist effort.

The need for a convention is pressing. It should not be regarded as another attempt in legal draftsmanship or as a futile effort to solve difficult problems by legalisms. It is a practical idea to create an effective instrument for coordinated action. For this idea to become reality, the United States must assume the leadership.

While a new international convention is still required, other international instruments warrant *reconsideration*. These conventions increase the danger to the life and safety of innocent civilians by extending the protection of the laws to terrorists and by treating them as equal in status to recognized combatants.

Better protection of non-combatants and innocent civilians against the dangers of war is a main goal of the rules of war. As early as 1874, the Declaration of Brussels, a historic cornerstone of the modern law of war, established the categories of people qualifying as combatants. They not only had to belong to a party to the conflict; they had to satisfy *four main conditions*, developed over many conferences and formalized in 1949 in the Third Geneva Convention (Article 4A2): First, they had to wear some distinctive article recognizable at a distance. Second, they had to carry their arms openly. Third, they had to have a commander. Fourth, they had to behave according to the generally accepted laws and customs of war.

The first two conditions emphasize what is called the Principle of Openness. Terrorists are thus clearly violators of international law, as they do not wage war openly. According the rights of combatants to those who do not fight openly endangers all civilians. And, in fact, the humanistic aim of protecting the innocent, the basis of all previous international law, has given way to the aim of protecting guilty terrorists. I am referring here specifically to the Protocol Additional to the Geneva Convention agreed upon in Geneva in July 1977. In one of its articles (44[3]), it radically departs from the Principle of Openness:

> In order to promote the protection of the civilian population from the effects of hostilities, combatants are obliged to distinguish themselves from the civilian military operation preparatory to an attack. Recognizing, however, that there are situations in armed conflicts where, owing to the nature of the hostilities, an armed combatant cannot so distinguish himself, he shall retain his status as a combatant, provided that in such situations he carries his arms openly. [He is required to do so] during each military engagement, and during such time as he is visible to the adversary while he is engaged in a military attack in which he is to participate.

In other words, the requirement of openness has been restricted to the stage of the *actual* use of arms the moment a grenade is thrown or a trigger pulled.

There is a basic inconsistency here. The opening provisions of Article 44 explicitly state that outward and apparent distinction of combatants is mandatory *to protect civilians*. But far from protecting civilians, the provisions adopted in the second part of Article 44 permit those who attack civilians to camouflage themselves. The principle of openness is not merely a formal requirement. It is vital for humanitarian reasons, for it maintains the distinction between combatants and non-combatants, and thus protects the civilian. Many legal authorities have pointed this out. Let me quote from three who have reduced the problem to its essence. Professor Denise Bindschedler, for example, states: "The guerilla must mark himself off from the civilian population whose fate becomes uncertain when every civilian may be suspected to be a camouflaged guerilla."*

Professor Draper, the British expert on the law of war, has put the matter this way: "Once the . . . man with the bomb who is a civilian in all outward appearances but can blow you to smithereens as you pass him by, once you bring such a person within the framework of the protection given to regular armed combatants under Article 4 of the Geneva Prisoners-of-War Con-

---

* D. Bindschedler, "A Reconsideration of the Law of Armed Conflict, Conference on the Law of Armed Conflicts, Contemporary Problems," Carnegie Endowment for International Peace.

vention, you make life for every single civilian hang upon a thread . . ."*

Professor R. R. Baxter voiced a similar opinion: "If persons attempt to take advantage of the protection given to those who do not fight in order to commit belligerent acts, then they jeopardize the position of the civilian population as a whole. The requirement of openness on the part of those who fight is the linchpin of the protection of civilians. If the distinction is abandoned, every civilian may become subject to attack, not as a matter of law but as a matter of fact. But the law will crack under blows of fact."†

Dispensing with the requirement of openness means overlooking the essential need to protect civilians, on which the whole humanitarian structure of the law of war rests. Doing precisely that in an attempt to curry favor with the state supporters of terrorists was the motive of many governments who supported this provision of the 1977 Protocol. Confusion was another. Promoting international cooperation in an anti-terrorist convention and rejecting compromises in humanitarian law should be among the foundations of the international effort to combat terrorism.

---

* Statement at ICRC Istanbul Conference, September 11, 1968.
† Proceedings of the International Symposium on Humanitarian Law, Brussels, December 12–14, 1974. *The Concept of International Armed Conflict*, p. 5.

VII

THE DOMESTIC BATTLE

ALTHOUGH TERRORISM has been increasingly an international problem requiring international measures, much can be done to fight terrorism *within* each country attacked by terror. Terrorists can be tracked down, tried, and punished. The movements and activities of potential terrorists can be observed, and they may be apprehended before they act.

Two questions are often asked when Western societies consider such actions: Can these measures work within a democracy? Do they pose an intolerable threat to civil liberties?

The answers to both questions may be found in the actual experience of democracies facing these challenges. Italy, Britain, Israel, and West Germany have been the democracies most assaulted by terrorists in recent decades. Yet each has been able to curb, and at times even reverse, the spread of terrorism within its borders. While terrorism has not been completely eliminated in these countries, its effects have been minimal. Terrorists have not plunged these societies into chaos and have not induced a change of government. Many terrorist organizations have been dismantled or put on the defensive, and terrorist demands have been largely resisted.

This has been achieved mostly by the existing police and legal powers. In some cases, special authority (deriving either from existing or emergency legislation) was invoked during crises.

Governments also trained their police and security forces to fight terrorists, monitoring budding terrorist groups and developing military techniques to thwart terrorist attacks, especially the taking of hostages.

The main point is this: In none of the liberal democracies has the adoption of such strong anti-terrorist measures led to a significant or lasting curtailment of individual freedoms. Often the measures adopted resembled, or were identical to, those used against organized crime. Indeed, the point of departure for the domestic battle against terrorism is to treat it as a *crime* and terrorists as *criminals*; to do otherwise is to elevate both to a higher status, thereby undermining the ability of governments to fight back. On the domestic level, the fact that terrorists are *politically* motivated criminals is irrelevant, except in providing clues for their apprehension.

The Five Tiers of Domestic Action

EDWIN MEESE III

IN DEVELOPING A STRATEGY to counter terrorism, governments must consider five elements: preparation, prevention, operation, adjudication, and education.

Preparation requires that governments formulate policies for fighting terrorism. They must clearly delegate the responsibility and authority needed. This is particularly important in the United States, where many agencies are involved in the task of fighting terrorism. Governments must also make certain critical decisions on how they will behave in emergencies. To ensure a level-headed policy, such decision should be taken *before* rather than *during* a crisis. For example, what will our policy be in hostage situations? Will we emphasize a flexible response, a guaranteed safe release, or a no-concessions policy?

In confronting a terrorist crisis, a government necessarily has to balance opposing objectives. It wants to be in control, to make no concessions, to end the situation swiftly, to save hostages, to apprehend the terrorists, to minimize political damage, and to avoid appearing callous or inhumane. Since these objectives cannot be fully reconciled with one another, the government must establish unmistakable priorities.

Equally, we must develop guidelines on the use of force and on the release of information to the news media in order to avoid indecision or ambivalence in the face of armed threats.

Plans must be worked out in advance to meet the maximum

range of foreseeable contingencies. Training is indispensable, the kind that was so evident at Entebbe. And exercises are needed to test the training, the planning, and the policies.

Rule of law and respect for democratic values and processes must be at the basis of all preparation. The underlying objective in countering terrorism should be the maintenance of democracy. It is not necessary to give up constitutional government and the rule of law; indeed, that is our bulwark in successfully combating terrorism.

Prevention of terrorism begins with a political climate in which it will be difficult for terrorists to develop an infrastructure for refuge and support. But prevention also means all-important intelligence. Adequate intelligence *can* be gathered in a democratic society by legitimate means without infringing on people's freedoms. Information must be sought aggressively and then shared between domestic (and international) agencies. Our statutes should not prevent the mutual exchange of intelligence information with other nations. Prevention also means denying access to terrorists. By sharing information with other governments and by improved control of our borders, we can stop terrorists before they enter the country. And we must reassess the whole question of diplomatic immunity so that terrorists will be unable to enjoy the support of diplomats, diplomatic facilities, or diplomatic pouches. Finally, prevention means denying opportunities to terrorists. Their likely targets must be protected. Such arrangements have been put into effect at the White House, the Capitol, and other federal buildings, and more are necessary. With minor inconveniences, the public remains free to come and go, but the terrorist's job is made considerably more difficult.

Operation is the third element of counterterrorism. Once terrorists strike, the attitude the government adopts is decisive. Officials must be calm, in control, and prepared to provide full support to the police, the military, and the security agencies. Above all, government officials must prevent the terrorist from achieving his objectives. For once the terrorist has launched his attack, there are three ways he can win: (1) If he gains his demands, he has won a victory over the government and over society. (2) If he commits an atrocity and gets away with it, he has promoted fear and demoralized his opponent. (3) If he provokes the government to overreact, he might induce resentment in the general public and promote further terrorism. The authorities therefore must deny the terrorist his demands, limit the number of his potential victims, and maintain the framework of the rule of law.

Adjudication comes in when a terrorist or his supporters are apprehended. Justice requires that any terrorist who is caught be brought to trial. For example, people everywhere have been impressed with the meticulous investigation undertaken by the Italian authorities into the assassination attempt on the Pope. Nothing is more frustrating and damaging than to apprehend a terrorist, only to find him able to defeat the criminal justice process because the law-enforcement authorities failed to gather the necessary evidence.

Education is the last critical task of government. The public must be educated about the real nature of terrorism. During a terrorist incident, the authorities must accurately present facts to the public. They must make it clear that terrorism is not idealism but pure crime. The terrorists must be portrayed neither as oppressed misfits nor as romantic revolutionaries but as the criminals they are. It is also important to demystify the intimidating image of the terrorist. With few exceptions, there are virtually no terrorists who are fanatic enough to be impervious to normal feelings of fear. Overwhelmingly, terrorists do *not* want to die for their cause and, given the opportunity, they will surrender. The terrorist is not a giant ten feet tall.

There is no panacea in combating terrorism. We have available to us a range of means to do the job—laws, government agencies, procedures, and experience. We can be effective if we adapt these means to the specified requirements of the war against terrorism, and if we have the will to use them.

Fighting Terrorism in the United States

WILLIAM H. WEBSTER

THE FBI has the principal responsibility for countering terrorism in the United States. This includes both international and domestic terrorism. International terrorism refers to terrorist acts in this country with foreign funding or direction or which extend beyond our border. Everything else is domestic terrorism.

Combating this form of lawlessness presents special obstacles for democracies, which by their nature wish to preserve basic freedoms. Indeed, if we respect these freedoms completely, it may be impossible for us to totally eliminate terrorism. We know we cannot stop every terrorist threat; as long as a single terrorist is free, widespread death and destruction remain real possibilities. There is no absolute solution.

Moreover, terrorists who once operated in small and independent groups have increasingly received help from countries which provide them with money, training, weapons, encouragement, and refuge. But free societies have tremendous resources and, at least in the United States, a growing resolve to control terrorism.

Within the United States, there is not so much a rising tide of terrorism as a rising concern about it. In light of the spectacular attacks throughout the world, that rising concern is understandable.

Yet there is good evidence that law-enforcement agencies can significantly reduce terrorism. For example, in 1982 the FBI arrested five terrorists from the Justice Commandos for Armenian Genocide for attempting to bomb the Turkish consulate in Philadelphia. Later that year they arrested three terrorists of the Armenian Secret Army for the Liberation of Armenia (ASALA) for attempting to bomb an Air Canada building in Los Angeles. This was a severe blow to the Armenian terror network in the United States, although the danger from that source persists. We mounted similar efforts against our most violent domestic group, the Puerto Rican FALN. That same year, 1982, the FALN committed twenty-five terrorist acts. Intelligence reports warned that they were planning more bombings, and robberies, as well as extricating imprisoned FALN members from various prisons, an important symbolic act to this group. We watched them, literally; we listened to their plans, literally; and after eighteen months, just as they were getting ready to move, we arrested four of their leaders. We also obtained information that allowed Mexican authorities to arrest FALN member Willie Morales, another leader of the FALN movement. The result was that in the following year the FALN did not claim responsibility for a single incident, and there were only three Puerto Rican–related incidents.

The largest number of the FBI's investigations concern international terrorism. Our counterintelligence guidelines govern the approaches and the techniques that we may use. The Foreign Intelligence Surveillance Act establishes what we need to show in order to undertake sensitive investigative techniques such as electronic surveillance. This act has been particularly helpful to us because it has eliminated concerns that often arise when there are no rules to go by. The guidelines have, in fact, reinforced protection for individual liberties.

Investigations of domestic terrorist groups are handled much the same as investigations of criminal enterprises, simply because crime is always involved. They are conducted under the Attorney General's guidelines for general crimes and racketeering. These investigations not only require a determination of who committed terrorist crimes but also how the perpetrators relate to other criminals, how they are financed and supported, and who their leaders are. In the course of these investigations in recent years, we have found more revealing relationships. We are now able to focus on the entire terrorist network rather than on what a particular group decides to call itself. We have developed a research and analysis center at FBI headquarters to analyze and computerize data on terrorists active in the United States.

We also cooperate with other law-enforcement agencies. Jurisdiction over terrorist crimes is often shared by state and local agencies. We have established several joint task forces on terrorism, particularly with the New York City Police Department. We have made special preparations for public events that might offer attractive targets for terrorists, such as the Los Angeles Olympics of 1984. A principal addition to our capability in recent years has been the Hostage Rescue Team, trained to act in cases when hostages are taken.

For years Americans as individuals have been a favorite target of terrorists around the world. We are regarded as an enemy by many countries and movements that use terrorism. Such enmity could bring terrorism to our shores. The mass media play a central role in our culture. The entire country can watch an event. We have large foreign communities that could form an effective base for terrorists. In short, all the ingredients are present for serious terrorist attempts within the United States. Still, because of its unique traditions, America offers an inhospitable political environment for terrorism.

But constant vigilance is indispensable. Aggressive and wideranging investigations of domestic terrorist activities must continue. The FBI's intelligence capability has significantly improved. But much needs to be done against the growing threat of international terrorism. Crises abroad in which America becomes intimately involved may well have repercussions here.

We have to keep the pressure up on all fronts. Our people are trained, motivated, and disciplined. They know their jobs and, equally important, the requirements of the law. All of us have worked hard to earn the trust of the American people and the international community, and we intend to keep it.

Fighting Terrorism in the Federal Republic of Germany

CHRISTIAN LOCHTE

THREE MAIN terrorist groups have operated in West Germany in the 1980s. The first two are left-extremist, the Red Army Faction (RAF) and the Revolutionary Cells (RZ); the third is the neo-Nazi Hepp-Hexel group.

The RAF operates underground as an urban-terrorist group. Since its beginning in the late 1960s, it has defined itself as Marxist-Leninist and as part of the "worldwide revolutionary movement." Until 1977 the RAF identified with movements in the Third World. Since then, however, it has focused its efforts against what it considers the world's two main imperialistic powers, the United States and West Germany. As a result, the RAF has tended to confine its activities to West Germany. Its particular targets are the staff and facilities of the American Army, NATO, and the national institutions and public figures of West Germany. The RAF carries out murders, kidnappings, and bombings, though it professes not to attack "innocent" citizens. Its only foreign contact that has been firmly established is with the PLO, in whose camps RAF members have undergone training.

Since 1973 the RAF has been operating a legal wing, which pursues its political goals openly. Observing and tracking persons involved on this level enables us to monitor the activities of the terrorists. Almost everyone who had belonged to the legal wing and then switched to the underground was traced by our agency before they took part in terrorist actions. The importance of intelligence surveillance of the *political* front of terrorism cannot be overestimated. Let me give just one example: In 1973 the Office for the Protection of the Constitution learned that the Trotskyite Group of International Marxists was splintering because of an internal dispute about relations with the RAF. Two members left the group. We kept both under surveillance because we considered them potential recruits of the RAF. We were proven right. They soon resurfaced as founders of a new terrorist group in Hamburg, nine of whose members were arrested on February 4, 1974. But despite these setbacks, the RAF is still active. It has attacked Americans and American facilities, mainly military ones.

The second group of left-extremist terrorists in West Germany is the Revolutionary Cells (RZ). It consists of small, independent groups of three to five members each. They do not live underground but lead a normal life, since their ideology requires that they participate in aboveground leftist politics. RZ ideology is "anti-imperialist" and "anti-Zionist." This means they attempt strikes at American and Israeli targets in West Germany. Since the 1970s the RZ has had an international section, with extensive links not only to the Palestinian Arab organizations but also to the IRA. Its members took part in well-known international acts of Arab terrorism, including the raid on the OPEC conference in Vienna in 1975. There has been no simple way of obtaining advance warning of RZ attacks. One approach is to monitor those RZ members who are openly active in New Left political organizations. Another is rigorous analysis of RZ pamphlets, which often indicate the inclination to actual violence of a given cell.

The third type of terrorist organization is the neo-Nazi Hepp-Hexel group. Curiously, it is the first such extreme right group to profess an "anti-imperialist liberation" ideology. Established in 1982 by Walter Hexel and Odfried Hepp, it consists of a few core members. In a 1982 pamphlet, *Farewell to Hitlerism,* Hepp and Hexel attempted to justify their "liberation struggle" against the United States, whom they regard as the main enemy. They distinguish between Eastern and Western imperialisms, concluding that the Soviet variety is positive, while the United States is viewed as occupying West Germany and imposing an alien democratic regime on Germans. Liberating West Germany from this oppressive rule mandates attacks on American facilities.

Soon after its formation, the Hepp-Hexel group went underground, financing itself through bank robberies. On December 14 and 15, 1982, it bombed three cars belonging to American soldiers in Hesse, seriously injuring two GIs. Solving these bombings proved very difficult. We knew at the time that neo-Nazi terrorists were espousing terror in general, under the slogan "The worse the better." Their aim was to horrify, as it was when they bombed the Munich Oktoberfest in September 1980, killing 13 persons and wounding 215. In the Hesse bombing we had preliminary indications of neo-Nazi involvement. We analyzed many neo-Nazi pamphlets to discover which group might have a specific motive for attacking Americans. We found such a motive in the pamphlet *Farewell to Hitlerism,* and were thus able to trace the crime to the Hepp-Hexel group. It is probably also responsible for attacks against Israeli targets, since, characteristically, the group is a mixture of persons who were trained by Al Fatah in Lebanon and persons with a "nationalist Bolshevik" ideology.

Combating terrorism, therefore, requires an extensive understanding of extremist behavior. For terrorism cannot be viewed as detached from other expressions of extremism. As our experience has shown, we should meticulously analyze publications of terror groups, thereby identifying their unique ideology, political arguments, logistics, targets, and actions. But we must begin with the understanding that, for terrorist groups, *all* actions are politically motivated.

VIII

THE GLOBAL BATTLE

THE FIGHT against terrorism cannot be limited to domestic measures alone. As terrorism has been adopted as a method of warfare waged by governments and their proxy groups, it is increasingly an *international* problem and must be addressed *internationally*. The actions needed must be directed not only at the actual perpetrators but at the terror organizations that launch them. This requires a policy of no surrender and a willingness to use force to thwart terrorist actions. But action must be directed also, perhaps especially, at those states that enable terrorists to operate across international boundaries.

In the Middle East, at least, full-fledged terrorist states have emerged; that is, regimes that employ terrorism as the principal weapon against their adversaries. Such states are the indispensable element in the growth of terrorism. Without them, terrorism would shrink to its former *domestic*, and hence less threatening, proportions. With them, it can grow to frightening dimensions. For these regimes can develop or obtain means of destruction—conventional, chemical, and nuclear—that the most sophisticated organization cannot. And if they come to believe that they can strike at their enemies with impunity, provided they use clandestine means like terrorism, they may well escalate the ferocity of their attacks or even fundamentally alter the nature of many kinds of armed conflict. It cannot be ruled out that the threshold of nuclear war may be crossed one day by the miscalculations of a leader of such a state. Imagine a Qaddafi or a Khomeini with nuclear weapons.

Unopposed, terrorism sponsored by governments poses a much greater threat to the West and to the entire world than has been commonly recognized. But precisely because governments are involved, the West can take effective action against this kind of terrorism. Many measures are possible—political, economic, and military. But none will be truly effective unless the major targets of international terrorism, the Western democracies, unite in concerted action.

What is required by the democracies is a recognition that terrorism against one of them is ultimately directed against all of them. The terrorists clearly see things in this fashion, and they are right. Terrorists and their backers are enemies of democracy. Success in one part of the world emboldens terrorists everywhere; and the weakening or collapse of a democracy, especially the seizing of power by the terrorists themselves, inevitably means the further spread of terror in the world. Only the democracies can undertake the global battle against terrorism. There is no lack of weapons. The crucial element is the summoning of will.

The Nuclear Terrorist State

ALAN CRANSTON

THE THREAT terrorism poses to the nations of the free world is immeasurable. Nowhere in the world is war raging with fewer restraints and more frequent resort to terrorist tactics than in the Middle East and South Asia. We have seen the death struggle between Iran and Iraq in the Persian Gulf. Contravening traditional rules of war, these nations used every possible weapon against each other. In the interminable conflict in Lebanon, the forces of terrorism and extremism thrive. And vicious civil strife across religious divides is growing in India and elsewhere in South Asia. International treaties have not barred the use of chemical weapons, attacks against diplomats, attacks on nuclear installations, attacks on religious sites, attacks on commercial shipping, even deployment of brigades of children as human "mine sweepers."

Terrorism, of course, has been a principal weapon of nearly all the regimes in this region. Its use has become synonymous with foreign policy. Little imagination is needed to understand the dangers posed to American national security and to the interests of our allies if such terrorist regimes and groups were ever to acquire nuclear weapons.

Does anyone doubt that if the Shah of Iran had succeeded in developing a full-fledged nuclear program in Iran, the Ayatollah Khomeini would have used a nuclear weapon against Iraq? Does anyone now doubt that if Iraq had been permitted to make swift progress toward a nuclear-weapons capability, Saddam Hussein would have used a nuclear bomb against Iran? Or that either of them might have resorted subsequently to a nuclear strike in a *jihad*, a "holy war," against Israel?

Those most concerned about the spread of terrorism and the use of weapons of mass destruction by terrorist states should be deadly serious about the need for a sound and successful nuclear non-proliferation policy. The democratic nations have clear responsibilities to check terrorism and to prevent terrorists from gaining access to weapons of mass destruction.

But the fact is that the industrialized democracies of the West have done grave injury to our security interests by widespread exporting of nuclear technology with military applications. Like Lenin's capitalists, who would sell the rope for their own lynching, we have permitted the export of nuclear material, plants, and technology that may someday be used in a lethal assault against us.

Several fundamentalist Islamic states have already made great efforts to develop nuclear weapons. In 1984 I revealed substantial new information demonstrating that Pakistan had acquired the necessary capability for this purpose. I cited four main points:

First, Pakistan had expanded its clandestine uranium enrichment facility at Kahuta; second, it had activated its clandestine plutonium reprocessing facility at PINSTECH; third, it had expanded its nuclear-weapons design team at Wah and stepped up imports of nuclear warhead components. And fourth, its KANUPP reactor's faulty safeguards made plutonium diversion highly feasible.

Pakistan had also developed the ability to export its nuclear-trained technicians, highly advanced nuclear technology and designs, and someday perhaps even nuclear weapons to other Islamic nations. This export capability and the extent of Pakistan's nuclear-weapons development poses an even more serious threat than Iraq's nuclear program before the bombing of the Osirak reactor in 1981.

Pakistan is a fundamentalist Islamic state. At the Islamic conference in 1981 (and again since then), it renewed its call for "holy war" against Israel. This is of obvious concern to anyone seeking to prevent nuclear conflict.

The West must consider the nature and practices of the regimes to which it exports nuclear technology. How, for example, did Pakistan get nuclear-weapons capability? It bought key components from Saint Gobain Techniques Nouvelles in Paris, VAT and CORA in Switzerland, Keybold Heraeus in West Germany, Emerson Electric in Britain, and hundreds of firms in the West who were so eager to make a sale that they chose to ignore Pakistan's unmistakable intentions.

The West, in fact, has repeatedly sold sensitive nuclear technology to countries which routinely employ terrorism as an instrument of state policy. How, to take another example, did Iraq come so close to attaining its own nuclear-weapons capability in 1981? It bought plutonium-producing reactors and weapons-grade enriched uranium from the French, and hot cells in Paris and Brussels, and it imported technicians from Italy.

And how did it put together the chemical weapons used with devastating effectiveness against Iran? It bought components from unwitting American firms. But the key ingredients for manufacturing its nerve gas apparently came from a firm that did know better, West Germany's I. G. Farben. Iraq has built up a chemical-weapons stockpile and production capability. It still possesses hot cells for reprocessing plutonium, a core load of at least 14 kilograms of highly enriched uranium, and a cache of more than 200 tons of raw uranium. It is working to rebuild the Osirak reactor. It has surrounded the reactor site with antiaircraft guns, balloons to frustrate low-flying aircraft, and 60-foot-high earth ramparts.

The nuclear program in Iran, begun by the Shah, was abandoned in 1979 by the Ayatollah as too reliant on the technology of the "satanic" West. This program has been revived. The Iranian Atomic Energy Commission was reconstituted; Tehran sent agents throughout Europe to press exiled nuclear scientists and engineers to return to Iran. Both lucrative offers and threats were reportedly made in an attempt to reassemble a team of nuclear specialists to work on a new, unmistakably Islamic, nuclear project. And representatives of the Iranian government approached firms in Switzerland and Belgium about plutonium-reprocessing technology. This technology could not be used by Iran for anything other than nuclear weapons; Iran has no genuine peaceful nuclear-energy program. It would take some fifty operating reactors before the peaceful application of such technology would even begin to approach cost-effectiveness.

In Libya, Qaddafi has for years tried to acquire nuclear weapons. He has pressed the Soviets to supply him with a plutonium-producing reactor. He has offered Pakistan cash and uranium in a nuclear trade. He has tried to buy nuclear weapons from China. At the very least, he is building the intellectual resources in Libya to help make weapons of his own. Libya's Tajura Nuclear Research Center offers use of highly enriched weapons-grade uranium. It possesses several extra core loads, though not enough for fabricating a nuclear warhead.

The Pakistani nuclear program is often touted as producing the first "Islamic bomb." It is fair to ask: Is it only Americans, Israelis, or Indians who believe this? Is this Pakistan's real intention? Concerns about the use of a Pakistani nuclear bomb in a "holy war" appear justified in light of the statements made by the program's architects. One must take seriously what Pakistan's leaders say. General Zia said: "China, India, the U.S.S.R., and Israel possess atomic arms. No Muslim country has any. If Pakistan had such a weapon, it would reinforce the power of the Muslim world." The late Prime Minister Bhutto wrote in his memoirs: "We know that Israel and South Africa have full nuclear capability. The Christian, Jewish, and Hindu civilizations have this capability. The communist powers also possess it. Only the Islamic civilization is without it, but that position is about to change."

Dr. A. O. Khan, the "father" of the Pakistani bomb, later charged that the "Islamic bomb is a figment of the Zionist mind and this has been used full force by the anti-Islamic Western countries." When he was convicted by a Dutch court for stealing sensitive nuclear-design information, he said that "all these charges and court cases were imposed at the insistence of Zionists and Western anti-Islam elements."

Pakistan is in a position to use its program as a magnet for training scientists from the several nations to whom it is in debt, like Saudi Arabia and Libya, or with whom it needs to curry favor, like Iran. Despite Islamization of Pakistan, involving public flogging, stoning, amputation, and the like, the Pakistani regime remains fearful of those in Pakistan who believe that the government has not gone far enough to advance fundamentalist causes.

Will Pakistani scientists help their fundamentalist colleagues in Iran and Libya, or even in the PLO? Will they export plans, designs, hardware, technology, or weapons-usable materials? The answers to these questions could have grave ramifications for American interests. They could affect the very survival of Israel. It would only take three nuclear weapons in the hands of terrorist groups or a government to destroy Israel. The United States thus has a compelling interest in preventing nuclear proliferation and nuclear terrorism. A regional nuclear war could swiftly bring in the superpowers and destroy us all.

There is much the democratic nations of the world should be doing. We should bar the sale of sensitive technology and dual-use hardware to unstable nations. We should halt aid to countries like Pakistan who are bent on developing nuclear weapons. And we should not sell them F-16s, the world's most advanced fighter-bombers, capable of carrying nuclear weapons.

For years, nuclear proliferation was a life-or-death threat that only a few talked about and warned about, but which no one did enough to stop. In the interim still another nation, Pakistan, joined the nuclear club.

We must face up to the ultimate terrorist threat. It warrants the urgent attention of the leaders of the West if we are to avert this grave challenge to our survival.

An International Agency
Against Terrorism

YITZHAK RABIN

THE FIRST HOURS of the Fourth of July, 1976, were the longest of my life. We were gathered in the command center of the Israeli army. Days of frustration and tension, during which we had failed to bring about the release of the hostages at Entebbe by diplomatic means, finally ended when the government of Israel reached a unanimous decision to send our troops to rescue the hostages.

The commandos landed. The first plane taxied to a halt at the place Yoni had chosen to disembark his unit. The assault started. Then the report came in; the terrorists were killed, the Ugandan forces were dispersed, the hostages rescued.

Our immediate reaction was an outburst of joy, and a sense of admiration for the men who had carried out the mission. Then came the sudden blow: Jonathan Netanyahu, Yoni, the commander of the assaulting force, was very seriously wounded. There were others wounded as well. And then came the worst news of all. Yoni had died.

Many of us knew Yoni, many more had heard about him. He was a leader of many battles. He had a unique nobility of character. He serves as an example of the best that we hope to find in our young generation: a man who devoted his life to the defense of his people and the values in which he believed.

We are taught by the long history of the Jewish people and

the short experience of Israel that there is no achievement without struggle, no joy without sadness, no light without shadows. Yet despite the terrible pain of Yoni's loss, Operation Jonathan at Entebbe serves as a landmark in the history of the free peoples' struggle against international terror.

The world today faces the danger of three types of war: nuclear war, conventional war, and international terrorism. The last is relatively inexpensive and highly effective in spreading fear. Fear of terrorism has become the normal way of life for many people all over the world, and governments are constantly trying to control it.

Why have we experienced the internationalization of terror? One reason is the cooperation among the various terrorist organizations in the last two decades. For example, eleven terrorist organizations based outside the Middle East cooperated with the PLO in its heyday in Lebanon, including the Japanese Red Army, the Montaneros, the West German Baader-Meinhof gang, the Italian Red Brigades, and the Irish IRA.

Another factor behind the growth of modern terrorism is the deepening involvement of sovereign states. Some states supply arms, sanctuary, and training facilities to the terrorist groups; others initiate terrorism directly. They all focus on the West, which has become the main target of international terrorism. The Soviet Union, for example, produced 95 percent of the PLO's weapons, most of which were shipped directly to Tripoli from Bulgaria. The United States, France, and Israel bore the brunt of the Shiite assaults in Lebanon.

The response to such international terror must also be international. Nations must find new ways of cooperating against the terrorist network. Let me give one celebrated example which illustrates the problem and points toward a solution. The terrorists who hijacked Air France 139 from Tel Aviv to Paris in June 1976 were Palestinian Arabs of the Wadi Haddad group and Germans of the Baader-Meinhof gang; they were supplied passports by an Arab country; they brought the plane and the hostages to Entebbe in Uganda; the government of Uganda and its armed forces assisted and protected the terrorists. This was a quintessential example of the two central features distinguishing so much of international terrorism: collaboration between terrorists from different countries and the direct collusion of sovereign states.

The first lesson of Entebbe is not to surrender to terrorism. Israel, in fact, was determined not to give in to the blackmail of the terrorists. But there was another, equally important lesson: the value of international cooperation in fighting terrorism. We were assisted by France and other countries in gathering intelligence. We carried out the operation on the assumption that the government of Kenya, without being notified in advance, would allow us to use Nairobi airport as a refueling station; without this, the operation could not have been carried out. Our assumption proved correct. The Kenyans did not even want to be reimbursed for the use of their airfield.

I propose that this type of cooperation be institutionalized and made concrete. Countries that choose to coordinate their activities against international terrorism should create a special international organization for this purpose. Obviously, this organization cannot be created within the framework of the United Nations. It can come into being only if the United States, the most powerful country in the free world, will take the initiative and call for its establishment. It will not replace the present bilateral arrangements that exist between Western countries. But without an international *center* that will direct and coordinate activities against terrorism, no real progress can occur in the war against terrorism.

This organization should coordinate four main functions: first, intelligence gathering and counterintelligence; second, protection of facilities and transportation routes. Scores and hundreds of lives have already been saved by cooperation in these two areas. Third, military operations in cases of emergency. There is no need to create new forces under the command of the organization; each sovereign state would control its own forces. But advance planning would enable combined operations when the countries involved agree to it. Fourth, and most difficult, political action against states that initiate and promote terror.

Countries that initiate terrorism must be made to understand that they will face an organized, united front of states, a union ready to take measures that an attacked country would not be able to undertake alone. The existence of such an agency might help serve as a deterrent, and possibly an effective means of sanctions and punishment. Its center should be in Washington. It should be headed by a senior American official and include permanent representation for all the member states.

The free nations need not wait for new outrages to unite in this effort. The time to act is now.

The Agenda
for International Action

PAUL LAXALT

INTERNATIONAL TERRORISM recognizes no national borders; its practitioners receive arms, money, training, haven, and political support from groups and governments. The victims of international terrorism are also not limited to the nationality that may be party to the conflict, and almost inevitably are citizens of different nations. Consequently, international terrorism must be fought internationally; it cannot possibly be defeated by the efforts of a single country, even by a superpower.

Since the beginning of the 1980s, the United States has been outspoken on this subject. But for America to be outspoken, even tough, is not enough. Many of the measures we have taken alone have been largely ineffectual because they were unsupported by others. The efforts of any one nation simply cannot inflict sufficient punishment on a terrorist state to make it change its policies. What is needed is a collective undertaking, not by some compromised and amorphous body like the United Nations, but by an organization similar to NATO, whose members organically belong to the West and share its values. Like NATO, established to deal with the threat of Soviet aggression in Europe, this body, consisting of the United States and Canada, the nations of Western Europe, Australia, Israel, and Japan, would be established to fight and defeat terrorism.

There are those who say we are doing enough and that no

modification of current policy is necessary. I believe that these people are wrong. The list of things I have to propose is neither exhaustive nor wholly original, but even the obvious has to be repeated until it is at last acted upon.

The first thing to understand is that collective action *does* matter. In fact, it makes all the difference. When there was a wave of airplane hijackings in the early 1970s, it was argued by some that nothing could be done. But once uniform security measures were adopted by the democracies, they did, in fact, work. In 1979, the Western powers issued the Bonn Declaration, making it clear that severe penalties would be suffered by countries that welcomed hijackers. As a result, the number of plane hijackings from Western airports was reduced significantly.

Terrorists tend to operate wherever they are tolerated. It is a serious mistake to suppose that they can be appeased. Rather than reward countries that treat them with deference, they make them their preferred field of operation. Terrorists treat accommodating countries the way a parasite treats a host, inevitably to the detriment of the latter.

Cooperation between governments for the expulsion or exclusion of terrorists and their supporters, even if they enjoy diplomatic immunity, is not enough. We need an extradition treaty among the members of the Western alliance, Japan, Australia, and Israel, committing each signatory to hand over to the others anyone wanted for acts of international terrorism.

We must increase our capacity to carry out retaliation and rescue. Secretary of State Shultz has said that we should not rule out preemptive strikes against terrorist groups *before* they attack. We do not need to be apologetic about this. If we learned that Libya or Iran had obtained, for example, a nuclear weapon, would we really be obliged to wait until that weapon was used? Or suppose we learned that a terrorist group was preparing to shoot down a civilian aircraft with shoulder-fired missiles. Would we really have to wait until the attack itself before taking action? That would be ludicrous. We have a right to defend ourselves before such would-be mass murderers attack us. What about retaliation? We should make our intention to punish the perpetrators of terrorist crimes unmistakable. Despite the difficul-

ties in finding them, we should make sure that when Americans
are attacked by terrorists we will punish the attackers and those
who supported them.

Economic sanctions have a bad reputation, but here again
concerted efforts can make the difference between futile ges-
tures and an effective nonviolent weapon. Most of the world
relies heavily on the Western economies. If we do not use our
economic power against terrorism, we may reach a point at which
the use of military power will become inevitable. And if used
wisely, that is, in coordination with our allies, our economic
power is awesome. Imagine, for example, Qaddafi's problem if
all the countries of the West simply withdrew their technicians
from Libya and refused to buy Libyan oil. Libya's oil production
would be crippled, and without Western customers its cash reserves would shrink drastically.

The entire world, including the Soviet Union, is dependent
on the West for technology and for goods and services that only
the industrialized democracies can offer. United, the democracies can achieve a formidable position. More often, the West's
experience has been one of disunity due to economic opportun-
ism and pusillanimity. A good example is again Libya. After its
agents murdered a British policewoman in London, the British
government severed relations with Libya, as the United States
had done a year earlier. Britain asked its allies in Europe to do
the same. But none did. Instead, many of them continued to
send delegations to Tripoli. This is not only a glaring case of
disunity but an unabashed race to benefit from an ally's distress.
Had the Western countries heeded the earlier call by the United
States for strong measures, Libya might have been considerably
more cautious.

We should not permit terrorist regimes and groups to enjoy
the privilege of international conventions, protocols, and treaties. For them, these are merely devices in their war against
the societies that uphold such agreements. By granting terrorist
states and organizations this kind of legitimacy, we are, in fact,
giving them a license to murder. By shutting down their embassies and offices, we can deny them the ability to abuse diplomatic immunity and diplomatic pouches.

Do we have the will, the strength, and the vision to take these steps? I believe we do. There are signs that the Western democracies are changing. Partly this is because of sensational terrorist attacks against the Western countries in recent years. Tolerance of terrorist groups, in whatever guise, has sunk to a low level, though it has not completely disappeared. Though some still feel constrained by the naïve and diseased sympathies of the past, the days are over when bank robbers and murderers masquerading as freedom fighters and liberators could capture the imagination of young people in the West. Most people have finally realized that terrorism is indefensible. They have also recognized that it is not a transient phenomenon. They understand that it is a new, protracted form of warfare against the West. The future of democracy requires that this onslaught of terrorism be defeated.

The Theory of Grievances

MIDGE DECTER

A PRINCIPAL PROBLEM in fighting terrorism is the notion that the grievances of terrorists may justify their actions. This idea is widely accepted by both active supporters and passive observers of terrorism. Let me give one example: On Third Avenue in New York City, outside the British consulate, and, as it happens, right around the corner from my office, for several years now a group of IRA sympathizers has been gathering every day in the late afternoon behind a police barrier. Under the eyes of two policemen the group parades up and down, screaming into a portable megaphone such sentiments as "British murderers in Northern Ireland must die." At first the passersby were curious. By now, years later, the group has dwindled to a dozen or so stalwarts, and passersby take their presence and their message entirely for granted. Few people stop anymore to ask them why they are there. Does anyone, for example, consider that these people might actually be on the payroll of Libya? The answer is no. Ordinary citizens, deep down, do not as a rule credit the idea that there are organized, cold-blooded murderers in the world. Then, too, these demonstrators have grown so boring that many have grown inured to what they represent. Tell the passersby that money and weapons being procured by the demonstrators for their comrades across the Atlantic are going for murders and bombings in London and Belfast and they would not believe you. They might even accuse you of seeking to deny civil liberties to the downtrodden.

I gave this example precisely because it is so minor, so normal, so harmless. It is thus a perfect illustration of the indifference to terrorism that has characterized so many tolerant people in our society. Some might argue that the inability to conjure up terrorist horror is a virtue of the democracies, deeply imbued as they are with the habits and traditions of civil decency; our very morality makes it difficult for us to recognize and resist terrorist crime. That Western societies are overly benign and decent is a tempting idea. In an important sense, it is true. Yet there is a darker and far less flattering truth about us as well. Unless we face it squarely, we may not only fail against terrorism but jeopardize our future and our freedoms: It is often not a higher morality that guides our actions but a moral and political surrender.

In the case of terrorism, this surrender takes the form of an almost automatic recourse to the theory of grievances. Terrorists, we are told, are groups or individuals with grievances. The IRA have theirs, the PLO have theirs, the Red Brigades have theirs, the Shiites have theirs, the Weather Underground have theirs. They are all motivated by some unanswered claims they make upon the world. What they do may be deplorable, goes the theory, but they have been driven to it by passions and yearnings denied and thus turned sour, bitter, and violent.

Yet it has become increasingly apparent over the years that terrorism is not some spontaneous response to social conditions, but organized political warfare. Why, then, is the notion of grievance-driven terrorism still so prevalent?

The theory of grievances is not a misguided effort to explain or understand terrorism. Rather, it is intended to deny the application of the normal moral code to the terrorist. Driven to murder by his inability to lawfully achieve his ends in an indifferent world, he is to be beyond the bounds of ordinary moral responsibility and judgment. Thus his acts of murder are not really murder and, above all, are not his. Murder, after all, is a willful and private action and punishable as such. The terrorist bombing of women and children on a bus is something else. It is a social disease. Terrorists are merely the carriers of this disease, rather in the way that innocent animals might be the carriers of rabies.

Behind this theory is a deliberate moral agenda. Deny a man normal human responsibilities and you no longer have to make a decision about him; he becomes a generalized societal misfortune, like a mine disaster or a power failure. And once you deny someone his moral responsibility for the consequences of his behavior, you conveniently relieve yourself as well of your own responsibility to act. The idea that terrorists embody or represent the interest of groups with grievances has freed many in the West from having to assume the burden of moral, political, and military action.

In failing to act, people may insist that they are really protecting higher values—freedom, for example. But values do not in fact come into it. There are no values when nothing, not even the prevention of bloodshed, is worth the risk of bloodshed.

To return to my neighbors on Third Avenue—each day they shout their obscenities, not only without fear of sanction, but, what is far more important, without fear of contradiction or argument. The day that no one dares or cares to name these people for what they are, accomplices in murder, is the day the democracies will truly have something to fear from terrorism.

Historians looking back on us from that dark world in which the light of freedom has been snuffed out will not say, "They were too good, and noble, and innocent, and freedom-loving to protect themselves." They will say, "They were too morally lazy to do whatever was necessary to keep their blessings alive for the rest of us."

A False Symmetry

JACK KEMP

LEO STRAUSS once wrote of behavioral scientists: "Rome burns while they fiddle, but they have two excuses: they don't know Rome is burning, and they don't know they are fiddling." Strauss could have been describing the way too many in the West look at terrorism today. They fail to understand what he believed was the basic question in politics: its moral dimension. We cannot truly understand international terrorism unless we see it for what it is—a profound political evil which the democracies must fight.

Though many now recognize the role of the Soviets in international terrorism, that does not appear to matter all that much. This fact is too often denied, or dismissed, or ignored; or the implications are lost in a fog of moral confusion. In the face of a mountain of evidence of Soviet involvement, many continue to deny its reality. It might be that they engage in what Owen Harries has called "best case thinking." That is the insistence on seeing the world through rose-colored glasses, on looking at the behavior of enemies of free societies in a way that explains away any real threat. Such thinking can disarm and blind us when it comes to dealing with the likes of Qaddafi or Khomeini, or the latest ruler in the Kremlin. For the most part, Western democracies have taken a business-as-usual approach to the sources of terrorism. They have failed to unite against terrorists and the states that back them. They have unwittingly given terrorists the legitimacy that they so eagerly covet by allowing their spokesmen and front men to walk unhindered through the capitals of the West, or to appear unchallenged on Western television; in other words, to exploit the opportunities that only free societies can provide.

In its struggle with terrorism, then, the West is handicapped by the ease with which terrorists manipulate us. But we put ourselves at a further disadvantage. It is not so much that an important part of Western political opinion is "soft on communism" or "soft on terrorism." Rather, it has become soft on democracy. This is best seen in the false symmetry so often adopted to describe the conflict between the West and its adversaries. Some say that America's liberation of Grenada was no different, for example, from the Soviet invasion of Afghanistan. Others say that United States support for those seeking to reestablish democracy in Nicaragua is no different from the Soviet efforts to topple the democratically elected government of El Salvador. It is as though they do not know of the political prisoners, the religious persecution, the censored press in Nicaragua; or that they have not seen the people of El Salvador standing for hours in the hot sun to exercise their right to vote. The Iranian Mujahdeen, the misnamed "Contras," the boat people of Cambodia and Vietnam, the members of Solidarity—these people have no problem recognizing the asymmetry between freedom and tyranny.

The democracies, too, must end the moral and intellectual confusion that has hobbled them. Evil *can* be distinguished from good. Democratic governments owe it to their citizens to make that distinction. For without it we are left defenseless against an enemy that relies precisely on the free world's tendency to engage in moral relativism, to blame itself for everything, and to justify the behavior of its enemies by ascribing to them its own motivations.

This false symmetry must now be discarded. The best place to start is with terrorism. It is one of the few politically motivated attacks that the public instinctively knows is absolutely alien to the character of democratic societies, that it is in fact *evil*.

Nothing can explain terrorism away. And nothing should permit others to compare us to terrorists. Thus, the war against international terrorism, essential in itself, will also help us to regain our moral clarity and our self-confidence. To fight against international terrorism, at bottom, means to fight for the fulfillment of our nature as free men and women.

Democracy versus Terrorism

JEAN-FRANÇOIS REVEL

INTERNATIONAL TERRORISM, mostly terrorism organized and manipulated by states, is one of the many tools totalitarianism uses to destroy democracy. It is triggered, masterminded, funded, and armed by the Soviet Union or its proxies. Outside the totalitarian world, terrorism flourishes, especially in the democratic West, which has been its main target during the past twenty-five years, and even more so during the past fifteen years. A quick survey demonstrates this.

Practically all the members of NATO have been attacked by international terrorism. Germany and Italy are well-known examples. The terrorist problem of Spain is less well known. There was, of course, Basque terrorism in Spain during Franco's regime. Basque terrorism during this period was often explained as a desperate resort to violence by a group lacking any other avenue for political expression. But oddly enough, the attacks increased and became more murderous *after* the democratization of Spain. This despite the autonomy established in the Basque provinces after free elections, an autonomy which granted the Basque region much more internal independence and freedom than, for instance, Quebec has in Canada. In reality, the Basque terrorists sought to topple the fledgling Spanish democracy. Their terror campaign was designed to provoke the army to attempt a coup. They nearly succeeded. The same pattern could be seen in South America. While authoritarian regimes have experienced terrorism, it is the democracies, especially the newly transformed ones, that have become the brunt of the terrorist onslaught. For example, when Venezuela returned to democratic rule in the early 1960s, Castroite terrorists attempted to assassinate President Betancur. In Argentina and Uruguay terrorists were more successful. Their actions led to the collapse of democracy in both countries and the establishment of military rule.

In their manifestos and books, the terrorists describe their attacks on democracies as the "strategy of tension." The idea is that it is much easier to go from fascism to communism than from democracy to communism. The "revolutionaries" must therefore first push the democratic governments toward a fascist pattern of behavior so as to build, in the second phase, socialism on the ashes of fascism. Usually the first part of the plan works magnificently, witness the case of Argentina and Uruguay. The same strategy was tried, abortively, in Italy and Spain. It is now being applied to Peru. For eleven years, from 1968 to 1979, Peru had a military dictatorship (admittedly a left-wing military dictatorship, one of whose achievements was reducing the gross national product by 60 percent). There was no terrorism. As soon as President Belaúnde returned to power through democratic elections in 1980, terrorism reappeared in full force and has escalated steadily since.

The main target of international terrorism is thus the democratic world. This underscores the asymmetrical relationship between totalitarianism and democracy. The terrorists, supported by totalitarian states, can operate almost freely among us; we do not even dream of promoting terrorism in totalitarian states. Some argue that terrorism, social unrest, and civil wars have reached such dimensions in the non-communist world because of our various failures and injustices. Whatever our shortcomings, the fact remains that the totalitarians and terrorists use our imperfections to destroy us from within. We cannot use theirs.

We fall into a trap laid by the terrorists and the totalitarians when we endorse the idea that we have no right to be free from attack unless we attain perfection, a duty they do not have.

Terrorism seeks to destroy its victims' political will. Worse, it is designed to make us accept the way the terrorists and the totalitarians see us. Terrorism, therefore, can best be understood as part of a global campaign aimed at the demoralization of the democracies.

What can we do to remedy this situation? First we must realize that fighting terrorism poses a problem of external defense, not only one of internal law and order. It is irrelevant to ask whether we endanger democracy if we fight terrorism with appropriate means. Second, our defense has to be collective, coordinated by all democratic countries. Third, we must stop making exceptions for terrorists, whatever the causes they claim to espouse. For many years, France had a tendency to consider Italian or Spanish terrorists as freedom fighters. Though indignant about France's benign attitude toward Spanish terrorists, Spain at one point invited Tony Negri, the Italian terrorist leader, to speak in Madrid about Marx. During the worst period of terrorism in West Germany, the radical intelligentsia in France, led by such figures as Jean Genet and Jean-Paul Sartre, explained that since West Germany was a fascist country it was perfectly normal for it to be punished by the Red Army Faction. Fourth, we must understand that terrorism is not an isolated phenomenon. It is part of the Soviet Union's program of global domination, a program that includes among its interim objectives the achievement of military superiority, the promotion of one-sided doctrines of non-interference, the domination of the Socialist International and the non-aligned movement, UNESCO, and the World Council of Churches, and the waging of systematic disinformation.

We must therefore stop considering terrorism a purely leftist *domestic* phenomenon. This change in our attitude and the policy that will result from it will not lead to a dangerous confrontation. It is weakness that invites aggression; the more the Soviet Union sees that its methods of destabilizing the democracies are easy to implement, the more dangerous our situation will be. Historical experience shows that the Soviet Union never persists in a given course once it understands that it cannot achieve its objectives at an acceptable cost.

Terrorism: How the West Can Win

BENJAMIN NETANYAHU

WHY SHOULD the West concern itself with terrorism? Its victims are few, its physical damage limited, its violence sporadic. In comparison with outright war, it poses a relatively minor threat to the lives and property of the citizens of free societies. Yet terrorism cannot be dismissed so easily. For one thing, it is escalating. The number and scope of attacks is steadily increasing. Aircraft are commandeered, passenger ships seized, politicians assassinated. Anyone is a potential victim. And while the number of those actually involved may be small, the entire world is set on edge—or rather, the democratic world, the West, the principal target of terrorism.

Free societies are naturally concerned with the welfare of their citizens in distress. And this concern is not necessarily related to the number of victims. A mine explosion, for example, may involve a handful of miners trapped underground, but the attention of an entire nation may be riveted to their fate for days, even weeks. This is not only because the cameras may be there to record the unfolding drama. There is a deeper reason. Consciously or unconsciously, every citizen imagines himself trapped in the same predicament. Will the rescuers get there in time or will he be abandoned to the forces of nature, forces beyond the reach of the authorities? It is the empathy for one's fellow citizen and the concomitant test of a government's ability to offer succor that endow these events with their importance to society as a whole.

Terrorism induces a similar anxiety—with one important difference. Unlike natural catastrophes, terrorism is neither purposeless nor fortuitous. It is deliberately planned, organized, initiated, and launched by people who wish to dramatize the powerlessness of governments. For whatever their specific motives or demands may be, the overriding consideration of all terrorist acts is to humiliate governments and expose their impotence. And this impotence is dramatized with special force and acuity when a handful of people are able to strike at anyone, anywhere, anytime.

The result is a loss of confidence on the part of the ordinary citizen in the resolve and competence of his government. To illustrate the crucial difference in the response of citizens, consider the reactions of people after a natural disaster like a hurricane or a volcanic eruption. The government's performance is seldom the predominant issue. Most people recognize, indeed accept, that a force of nature can wreak destruction beyond the capacities of government to prevent or immediately repair. After the initial anxiety, the common response is seldom anger but compassion, understanding, and a willingness to help. This is true even if the disasters are relatively frequent and serious, as in earthquake-prone regions. But persistent attacks of terrorism produce an entirely different reaction. The initial shock is transformed into criticism and rage at the government for not acting to prevent or curb such attacks. People instinctively agree with Churchill's dictum that a government's first obligation is to protect its citizens. While they may not always apply this standard in the case of natural calamities, they *always* apply it, stringently, in the case of armed attacks. The citizen points an accusing finger at his leaders, as if saying: I've entrusted you with the supreme obligation of protecting me and given you the exclusive authority and means to do so. You have failed. You have broken my trust.

Having induced in the public a sense of the government's impotence and of his own invincibility, the terrorist now reaps the real reward. For the stage is now set for the second critical

phase in the terrorist strategy—the consideration of his demands. I do not mean only the immediate ones (safe passage,
money, publicity, release of jailed terrorists, etc.), but the larger
political claims that he professes to represent. The citizens or,
to be more precise, the media, now press the authorities to
consider the terrorist claims. The citizens in effect turn to the
government and say: You have failed to stop the terrorist. He
is not going to go away. Listen to him, negotiate with him, give
him what he wants to make him stop.

This is a no-lose proposition for the terrorist. If the government does not give in, the terrorist promises (and often delivers)
further terrorism. This induces further criticism of the government and more, increasingly desperate calls to heed the terrorist demands. If the government succumbs, the terrorist
scores an obvious victory; even if the terrorist agrees to a temporary hiatus (which he seldom does), the citizen knows that his
government has caved in and betrayed his trust yet again. Like
a child clamoring for forbidden toys, the public expects the
government simultaneously to give in and to hold fast. And
once the line of concession is crossed, more atrocities and
more demands are sure to follow, with the inexorable logic of
blackmail in the face of weakness. The more outrageous the
attack, the more outlandish the target, the better. To call terrorist murders "senseless," then, is to miss the point. They are
anything but that.

The terrorist's strategy is premised on the ability to deliver
future blows, no matter what. The fear and intimidation that
terrorism thrives on is totally dependent on the ability to live
up to this threat. It is essentially the same kind of terror that
every person experiences during childhood in the face of the
neighborhood bully. As in the case of the bully, the necessary
response is twofold: the conscious refusal to be intimidated and
the willingness to fight back. Virtually always, this resolve has
to be demonstrated in action. The same is true of the terrorist.
Through repeated blows, he must be taught that his victim will
not only resist his assaults but fight back vigorously.

The terrorist objective, of course, is not negotiation but capitulation. As long as he can sustain the pressure, as long as he

can launch attacks with increasing frequency and audacity, he will advance toward his goal. The primary task, then, in fighting terrorism is to weaken and ultimately destroy the terrorist's ability to consistently launch attacks. This is often presented as a difficult or even impossible task. It is asserted that the clandestine nature of terrorism and the openness of Western societies make terrorism against the West nearly impossible to root out. I would argue the exact opposite. Terrorism can be easily stopped. The minute you weaken its ability to deliver repeated blows, you have broken its back. And it is well within the means of the West to achieve this. But before discussing the political, military, and other ways in which this can be done, we must consider further the moral debilitation which terrorism produces in our societies. For without an appreciation of the moral issues involved in the battle against terrorism, an effective defense is doomed.

What are the moral wounds that terrorism has already succeeded in inflicting on our societies? As we have seen, the number of victims and the extent of physical damage is not the issue. Rather, it is the shaken confidence in government, the questioning of its abilities and competence to ensure a world subject to the rule of law, and the way terrorism gradually *conditions* us to lawlessness and outrage. We are by now almost resigned to attacks on airline offices, seizure of embassies, hijacking of airplanes, bombing of government buildings, assassination of political leaders, machine-gunning of children. If as recently as the mid-1960s somebody had offered such a description for a world ostensibly at peace, we would have scoffed. Yet the realization that wild beasts prowl our airways and waterways, that they can escape retribution by fleeing to countries which respect, indeed worship, the law of the jungle, has been steadily replacing our older conception of justice, order, and accountability in international affairs.

In a curious way, straightforward war, even when launched for the most vicious motives, never did this. Such wars have clear terms of reference. They have a beginning, they have an end (even though that end may be a protracted one). The aggressor either loses, in which case our sense of justice is reinforced, or he may win, in which case we absorb the defeat by drawing a mental (and sometimes physical) demarcation line for the next battle, in the hope that the combination of defense and diplomacy will prevent it from breaking out, or failing that, from overwhelming us. There may be tragedy, but there is no moral confusion.

But terrorism does not offer us this comfort. Like an open wound that is constantly gashed, its relentless attacks continually open up new battlefields. No areas of life seem to be immune from its onslaught. For example, having finally gotten used to the idea that airplanes are unsafe, we have had to adjust (after the *Achille Lauro* piracy) to the new fact that cruise ships are targets too.

Terrorism not only cuts across political boundaries with apparent impunity. It violates our most precious moral and ethical boundaries. For the deliberate targeting of innocent civilians—shoppers, tourists, passengers, students—has gradually eroded the crucial distinction between combatant and non-combatant. It is not only that the terrorist breaks down this distinction. It is that *we* begin to accept his standards. With each fresh terrorist attack, the public is conditioned—first by the terrorists, then by his own compliant interpreters in the press—to equate innocent hostages with jailed terrorists and to accept the notion that the murder of children is a regrettable but understandable expression of the terrorists' purported grievance.

The distance from "understandable" to "legitimate" is a short one. It is made even shorter by the tendency of Western diplomacy, echoed by the media, to fall back on two platitudes concerning terrorism.

The first is the ready acceptance of the terrorist argument that even the most abhorrent violence is the direct result of certain "root causes," such as poverty, political oppression, denial of national aspirations, etc. But terrorism is not an automatic result of anything. It is a choice, an evil choice. That this is true can easily be seen in the many modern instances of the direst oppression, when the oppressed rejected terrorism and chose to wage their struggle by honorable means. Earlier in the book I cited a classic illustration of this principle, but because of its clarity it is useful to repeat it: No resistance movement in Nazi-occupied Europe conducted or condoned terrorist attacks against German civilians, attacking military and government targets instead. But today's terrorists need the flimsiest pretexts to perpetrate their crimes, targeting the innocent with particular relish.

The root cause of terrorism lies not in grievances but in a disposition toward unbridled violence. This can be traced to a world view which asserts that certain ideological and religious goals justify, indeed demand, the shedding of all moral inhibitions. In this context, the observation that the root cause of terrorism is terrorists is more than a tautology.

The "root cause" argument is especially popular in explaining away PLO and other Arab terrorism. That this terrorism was already raging during the 1920s, decades before the current grievances of Arab terror even existed (territories controlled by Israel after 1967 or, earlier, Arab refugees), is overlooked. Recently, a new variation has been introduced. It is argued that the absence of progress toward a peaceful settlement between Arabs and Israelis induces terrorism. The truth is exactly the reverse. Arab terrorism is not the result of breakdowns of peace negotiations; it is, more than any other factor, the *cause* of such breakdowns. (Arab leaders showing the slightest inclination toward peaceful coexistence risk immediate assassination by the terrorists.)

The second platitude blurring the true nature of terrorism is the "cycle of violence" argument, raised whenever governments contemplate action against the terrorists. It is proffered not only to warn of a possible practical consequence—an ensuing spiral of violence (an argument I will address later)—but as a moral injunction as well, i.e., responding to the terrorists with force lowers one to their level. As if military strikes aimed at the terrorists and terrorist attacks on civilians belong on the same moral plane. They do not. Safeguarding that distinction is central to prosecuting and winning the war against terrorism. For the terrorist's ultimate victory is to control our thinking and to assign the term "terrorists" to those of his victims who fight back.

Terrorists have been successful in propagating this false symmetry because of the sloppiness of the West's thinking about the use of force. America's loss of clarity in the wake of Vietnam has become a general Western malaise. The rules of engagement have become so rigid that governments often strait-jacket themselves in the face of unambiguous aggression. I am not suggesting that prudence and proportionality are any less relevant today in deciding on a response to aggression. They are not. Governments must weigh the political and military effects of their actions, even when they are fully justified. When dealing with a wave of repeated attacks like terrorism, they must judge whether to respond at all, when to do so (for example, after each individual incident or after an accumulation of attacks), with what means, and, of course, against whom (the terrorists, their back-ers, or both).

These questions, however, should not obscure a fundamental principle: Under no circumstances should governments *cate-gorically rule out* a military response simply because of the risk of civilian casualties. There is a practical and a moral basis for this position. In practical terms, an inflexible rule against risking civilian casualties would make any military action virtually im-possible. (This brings to mind Edward Luttwak's memorable observation that the only sure exception is aerial combat over Antarctica.) Knowing our inhibition, the terrorist would go to even greater lengths to put civilians at maximum risk. In moral terms, an absolute prohibition on civilian casualties today con-demns to death or injury many future victims of a terrorism that, undeterred, will inevitably increase.

Responsible governments seek to minimize civilian casualties. But they do not grant immunity to an aggressor simply because their response might endanger civilians. If this is true in normal combat, it is truer still in the case of terrorism. An absolute prohibition on civilian casualties affords the terrorist an invin-cible shield. This is not only true in cases in which he fears retaliation following his attacks (when the terrorist seeks im-munity by planting his bases among civilians). It is also true during the classic terrorist operation, the taking of hostages, when the terrorist even more brazenly seeks immunity by daring the authorities to take action and risk the lives of innocent vic-tims.

* * *

Why have I called hostage-taking the classic terrorist act? More than any other type of terrorist violence, it reveals two underlying characteristics of terrorism. First, it is an unmistakably *deliberate* assault on the people who are seized, precisely because they are noncombatants and outside the pale of acceptable conflict. There is simply no way to argue that the victims are accidental, as terrorists sometimes pretend when they bomb shops, airline offices, or other public places.

Second, it affords a stage for dramatization and distortion. The prolonged siege is one of the most effective ways in which terrorists propagate their message. Through media coverage and the negotiations to resolve the crisis, they seek to achieve legitimacy. What would normally be regarded as criminal extortion is transformed into a political act. It is important, therefore, to consider in some detail the appropriate response to the taking of hostages. For the principles that guide our response in this case pertain to all other forms of terrorism.

Hostage-taking places a government in a terrible dilemma: If it uses force to release the hostages, it might end up with more people killed than if it gives in. If it yields, the terrorists emerge victorious. Sometimes the terrorists resolve this dilemma by killing a few hostages and threatening to murder the rest if their demands are not met. The government can then argue that since more hostages are about to be killed anyway, it must take action immediately. But what if the terrorists do not begin killing their victims? Does that make a military response less necessary? The answer is no. The terrorist must believe that the authorities are prepared to take forceful action whether or not hostages have been killed. The mere act of *taking* hostages warrants such a policy. It is a fundamental error to let the terrorists believe there are instances when they are completely safe from military action.

The more terrorists believe that such action is likely, the less prone they will be to continue their siege. During the hijacking of the TWA airliner to Beirut and of the cruise ship *Achille Lauro* in 1985, a principal reason that the terrorists released their hostages was their belief in imminent intervention—retaliation afterward in the case of TWA, and military rescue in the case of the *Achille Lauro* (a correct assumption in the latter case, as both American and Italian forces were poised to storm the ship on the day the pirates surrendered).

The belief in the certainty or likelihood of military intervention has a tremendously inhibiting effect on hostage-taking. This is best demonstrated in the case of Israel. No nation suffered more from this form of attack. In the 1970s, Israel experienced a spate of hostage-takings, including the hijacking of planes and the seizing of schools, apartments, hotels, and buses. In all of these cases the government refused to capitulate to the terrorist demands. Soldiers overcame the terrorists and liberated the hostages. This was by no means an easy course to follow. The government painfully recognized that its policy made some civilian casualties unavoidable. Indeed, there were several cases in which hostages were killed. In one, Maalot, twenty-one schoolchildren were massacred by the PLO before the terrorists were themselves killed.

But what was the result of this determined refusal to yield? Incidents of hostage-taking gradually became a rarity inside Israel. This was not because the PLO was unable to stage such incidents; it is not particularly difficult to organize a handful of terrorists for this purpose. What limited the PLO's hostage-taking was the certainty that there would be no surrender and that the terrorists would fail and probably be killed. (Contrary to popular myth, cases of suicidal terrorism are rare; overwhelmingly, terrorists want to live, in fact, to escape unpunished.)

The PLO sought to overcome Israel's resolve by seizing Israeli planes or hostages outside Israel. But these attempts were defeated as well. The hijacking of Israeli planes or the taking of Israeli hostages anywhere became an extremely difficult proposition. For example, the hijacking of an El Al flight from London to Tel Aviv was foiled by security guards on board who killed one of the terrorists. In the most celebrated example, the case of Entebbe (1976), Israeli troops flew over 2,000 miles, liberated the hostages, and killed their captors. The effect on the terrorists was long-lasting. For a decade after Entebbe, not a single Israeli plane was hijacked, and virtually no attempts were made to seize Israeli hostages abroad.

The refusal to capitulate, and the decision to apply force, was adopted in several important instances by other governments. The German government forcibly liberated German hostages in the hijacked Lufthansa airplane in Mogadishu (1977), the Dutch successfully stormed a train hijacked by the South Moluccans (1979), and the British freed the occupied Iranian embassy in London (1980). For years afterward, these countries experienced no further hostage-takings. Experience shows that far from engendering a cycle of violence, the application of military force, or the prospect of such application, inhibits terrorist violence.

We can see this principle at work in the locations terrorists select to play out an act of hostage-taking. They choose places where they believe rescue is impossible. The hijackers of the Kuwaiti airplane landed in Tehran airport after killing two American hostages. In the TWA case, the Shiite gunmen deliberately brought down the airplane in Beirut airport, where the presence of heavy Shiite militia made rescue extremely difficult. In the case of Entebbe, the PLO hijacked the Air France plane to Uganda, where it was heavily guarded by Idi Amin's troops and was seemingly safe from any possible military action. In the case of the hijacked Egypt Air plane, the terrorists apparently chose Malta because they believed that the Maltese government, closely tied to Libya, would not permit a rescue attempt. The terrorists, in short, *fear* forcible intervention, and prefer to operate only when they think none will be forthcoming.

Given this reality, what should be the response of attacked governments? Clearly, the question should be one not of *policy* but of *means*. The only sensible policy is a refusal to yield and a readiness to apply force. This is a policy that in effect says to the terrorist: I will not yield to your demands. I demand that you release the hostages. If you do not do so peacefully, I am prepared to use force. I am proposing a simple exchange: your life for the lives of the hostages. In other words, the only "deal" I am willing to make with you is that if you surrender peacefully, I will not kill you.

Obviously, there can be complicating circumstances. What if military intervention truly does endanger the lives of most or all of the hostages? This is not quite as frequent as might at first appear. Many governments have specialized forces trained to overcome the terrorists before they kill most of their hostages. On occasion they fail, as was the case in the Egyptian rescue attempt in Malta and the Colombian government's decision to storm the terrorists occupying the Ministry of Justice in Bogotá in 1985. In both cases the decision to act was correct, whatever the operational consequences. But how to reduce the loss of innocent lives, an obligation that governments simply cannot ignore?

Rescuing hostages requires impressing on military forces the importance of *minimizing* firepower. In storming a building or an enclosed space held by an enemy, the normal military procedure is to shoot (or detonate) first and look later. But in rescuing hostages, the soldier's job is exactly the opposite: he must look first and shoot later, and even then only when it is absolutely necessary. This means that the rescuers must always put themselves at greater risk than they would otherwise do. They can, however, somewhat reduce the risk to themselves—and, more important, to the hostages—by repeated training and immersion in the accumulated experience of earlier rescues. This requires that special units, which over time develop expertise and perfect the techniques of rescue, be charged with liberating hostages. As the experiences of Israel, West Germany, Britain, and Holland show, more often than not, such units succeed. Still, one must face the stark reality that there are no guarantees of success and that a tragic loss of lives may indeed occur. Equally, there is no guarantee of failure. The military cliché is true: You can only be sure how a military action begins, not how it ends.

But let's take a case where the chances of rescue are faint or even nonexistent. Suppose the terrorists have not merely seized hostages but have hidden them? Perhaps the most celebrated case is the kidnapping of Italy's former Prime Minister Aldo Moro by the Red Brigades. Italy refused to capitulate and Aldo Moro was murdered. As tragic and as painful as the decision was, it was the right one, as was the firm Italian policy in the immediate aftermath of the Moro kidnapping. Unlike the weakness it later showed during the *Achille Lauro* affair, the Italian government mounted a vigorous effort to hunt down the Red Brigades and to improve the effectiveness of its security forces.

(By the time of the next major kidnapping, that of General James Dozier, it was able to apprehend the terrorists and liberate their hostage.) Whether or not such rescue is possible, governments must persist in refusing to capitulate. This is both a moral obligation to other potential hostages and, in the long view, the only pragmatic posture.

Once governments accept this principle, they can deal with other difficult cases. For example, what if the hostages are family members of government leaders? Terrorists sometimes target such relatives, betting that natural human feelings will override conviction. The personal agony notwithstanding, a leader placed in such a predicament should either refuse to give in or, what is kinder, delegate responsibility for making decisions in this matter to someone else.

Perhaps the most complicated case of hostage-taking is that in which the terrorists find refuge in the territory of a hostile country. Short of declaring war, what can be done? It is often difficult, though by no means impossible, to launch a limited military operation to rescue the hostages. In any case, the principle remains the same—refusal to yield, and the threat of intervention or retaliation. Retaliation can take several forms (against the terrorists themselves and the governments that shelter them). The main point to recognize is that both the terrorists *and* the government that shelters them must believe that they will eventually be punished (preferably sooner rather than later). Such a posture may not deliver the terrorists to justice, but at a minimum, it can secure the release of the hostages without any capitulation. This is essentially what produced the resolution of the hijacking of the Kuwaiti plane to Iran (1984) and the TWA hijacking (1985). When the *Achille Lauro* was seized by terrorists (1985), no government was willing to harbor the ship or the terrorists during the incident, because of a growing concern over some form of American retribution or sanction. The more terrorists and governments believe that they will be punished for taking hostages, the less likely it is that they will seize or accept them.

What is true of hostage-taking is true of other forms of terrorism. Whether it is hit-and-run killings or random bombings, the terrorist *always* considers, and fears, a forceful response from his victims. To the extent that he believes that he will be tracked down and punished for his actions, he will curb them. Deterrence works on terrorists just as it does on anyone else.

The cycle-of-violence argument is not only morally wrong; it flies in the face of actual experience. The terrorists may at first respond to a government's policy of firmness with an acceleration of terrorism, but they usually cannot withstand a sustained and resolute policy of resistance and active pursuit. Retaliation and preemption against terrorism are thus acts of self-defense.

Denying the necessity for such self-defense, and blurring the moral basis for it, is dangerous. It undermines a basic principle on which government authority is based. When a government shows weakness toward terrorists, citizens will demand action. If the government does not provide it, segments of the public might well turn to vigilantism and political extremism. Again, a government's first obligation is to protect its citizens. Confusion or vacillation, offered either gliby or high-mindedly, fool no one, least of all the terrorists.

But no policy, however clearly defined, will be worth much without the means and the resolve to carry it out. From everything that has been said so far in this book, one point emerges as central: International terrorism as we know it would simply not be possible without the collaboration of governments which have used terrorism to wage hidden war against their adversaries, especially the West.

These governments have not only supplied terrorists with the means to commit their crimes; they have also provided them with the all-important and indispensable assistance of safe passage and sanctuary. For the distinguishing feature of international terrorism is the perpetration of terrorist attacks across national frontiers. The terrorist must be *launched* from somewhere and he must *go* somewhere after his crimes. For example, in the aftermath of the *Achille Lauro* piracy, Abul Abbas, the mastermind of the operation, skittered from Egypt to Italy to Yugoslavia to Iraq to South Yemen, where he finally found his most suitable haven. Without the collusion or acquiescence of all these governments, he would have been caught and brought to trial. The support of friendly regimes, and the passivity of others, is the crucial assumption under which international terrorism operates.

Governments are not only at the root of the problem (the *internationalization* of terror) but are also the key to its solution. For states are no less susceptible than the terrorists they support to a sober calculation of costs and benefits. The very reason they rely on terrorists is to be able to wage war without the risks that war entails. As long as they are successful in denying complicity or involvement, they will easily escape retribution. But once their support of terror is revealed in such a way that the victims can no longer pretend to accept their denials, the rules of the game can change dramatically.

Once this is understood, the democracies can begin to act effectively in three broad areas against offending states.

First, there are political pressures that can be brought to bear. These could range from international condemnation to cutting off diplomatic relations (as the United States and Britain did in the case of Libya). Political pressures are important for several reasons. They signal to the terrorist state that the victim is not only unwilling to be compliant but is prepared to fully expose the offender to the light of public opinion. This could force other states to take a position against the offender, or at least to curb their support for it. Since many states sponsoring terrorism depend on the ability to deny complicity in terrorist crimes, this is not a minor threat. In the case of a severance of diplomatic relations there is an added penalty, the shutting down of embassies. The critical role of embassies, and the abuse of diplomatic privileges and immunities in general, in facilitating international terrorism has not been adequately appreciated. Terrorists simply cannot sustain a concerted campaign of attacks in most Western countries without sanctuary or inviolable means of passing funds, arms, and intelligence. Without embassies, the effectiveness of terrorism in the West would be sharply diminished. Imagine if the amateurish terrorists who kidnapped Patty Hearst could have fallen back on a network of diplomatic missions throughout the United States.

The embassies and diplomatic pouches of Syria, Iraq, Iran,

Libya, South Yemen, and other Middle Eastern states, as well as Soviet Bloc embassies, have turned parts of Western Europe into a veritable playground of terrorists. Weapons, passports, money, safe houses, indeed the full gamut of support, have been made available to terrorists by people hiding behind the designation diplomat and the protection offered by diplomatic immunity. Sometimes, as in the Libyan embassy shooting in London, they do away with the diplomatic masquerade altogether. When irrefutable proof links particular embassies to terrorism, they should be shut down. Offending states will be denied their fortresses of terror in our midst.

The second broad area in which the West can work against states which engage in terrorism is economic pressure. Most of these countries desperately need Western goods, weapons, or credit. There are certain sophisticated products, including advanced weapons, that only the West can supply. The combined purchasing power of the democracies is enormous. If the West used but a fraction of its formidable economic clout, it could cause regimes supporting terrorism to rethink some of their activities. Economic pressure could be a combination of boycott and embargo. For example, in the case of Libya, a prime offender, an effective policy would be: Don't buy and don't sell. Don't buy Libya's oil, don't sell it Western technology. Even a partial boycott and embargo has the effect, because of the need to go through intermediaries and brokers, of raising costs significantly. Of course, this often also has an effect on the countries which undertake these measures, and they must be prepared to shoulder such a burden. The United States, for example, has willingly forfeited hundreds of millions of dollars of trade with Libya in order to send an unmistakable message to that regime. Unlike the more difficult task of taking on a cartel, however, this kind of economic pressure isolates individual governments.

In addition to trade measures, there is another potent sanction that can be readily applied. It, too, has the virtue of not exacting a significant price from the West—the denial of landing rights to the commercial planes of terrorist states. Such states do not care if their planes can land in Moscow. What really counts is that their planes have the right to land in London, Paris, and New York. But if they use those planes to ferry terrorists (or their embassies to shield them, or their intelligence services to assist them), these states must know that their planes will not be able to land in the principal capitals of the West. The same could apply to docking rights for the ships of offending states.

May nations lawfully impose sanctions on other nations? They certainly may under any standard of international law, including the United Nations Charter. The fact that there have been repeated attempts in the UN to abuse this measure by applying it against innocent states does not vitiate the principle of sanctions itself. A resort to *mandatory* sanctions is a problematic concept, even though it was incorporated in the UN Charter for the best of intentions. Much preferable is the application of sanctions by a voluntary association of states.

Even without sanctions, the mere *withdrawal* of economic aid or other benefits that would otherwise accrue to governments which promote terrorism can have a sobering effect on them. Iraq, for example, made a conscious effort to curb some of the more egregious acts of terrorism it promoted in order to get itself removed from the State Department's list of nations supporting terrorism (though, as the provision of an Iraqi diplomatic passport and safe haven to the mastermind of the *Achille Lauro* piracy shows, this is by no means a rigorous Iraqi policy). Obviously, political and economic pressures demand a degree of unity among the Western countries. The ability to act in concert is paramount, an issue I will return to.

The third area of response by the West is, necessarily, military action. This cannot be ruled out, nor should we be bashful about discussing it. When we talk about using military force, we must first consider it in a unilateral context, that is, *one* state taking action against terrorists or a state that shelters them. Obviously, if a terrorist action occurs on a government's own soil, it will take action to foil the terrorists, whether during an actual incident (such as a hostage-taking) or on an ongoing basis. There is no question that a state has the right to act; the only question that is raised, and regrettably it is raised only in the West, is the problem of protecting civil liberties. Yet the experiences of Britain, West Germany, Israel, and Italy show that it is perfectly possible to combat terrorism effectively without any significant infringements on individual rights. The police, the security services, and the courts have done so by and large using existing legal procedures. The authorities have on occasion asked their legislatures to enact special, usually temporary and limited, legal measures. They have also created specialized military units to track down terrorists, though, as I have noted, these stress the minimal application of force. On the domestic level the approach to fighting terrorism in the democracies is the policeman's, not the soldier's; terrorism is basically treated as a variant of organized crime; the political trappings of terrorism are irrelevant.

But what about a terrorist attack on a country's citizens or installations abroad such as embassies, businesses, or airlines? Here the authorities face a stiffer problem. For the terrorists, by definition, are always under the jurisdiction of another government. That is so even in the case of piracy on the high seas or in the brief periods when a hijacked aircraft is aloft (a ship's or a plane's registry is, in the legal sense, its national identification outside national jurisdictions). I propose a simple way to resolve the question of conflicting jurisdictions: In the case of a hijacking, piracy, or other hostage-taking, the responsibility of securing the release of the hostages is the government's on whose soil (or ship, or plane) the incident takes place. One would hope such governments would adopt a firm policy against the terrorists, i.e., a refusal to yield and a readiness to apply force. Such governments should be held to this standard, at least to the first part, the refusal to yield. It is well within the means of the leading countries of the West to powerfully censure a government for failing to do so.

But suppose a government cannot or will not undertake to forcibly end a hostage crisis when the tactical negotiations have broken down. At that moment it forfeits a certain measure of jurisdiction over the event. The country whose nationals (or plane, or ship) are held hostage has the right to act when the host country refuses to do so. Take the case of Entebbe. Uganda had an obligation to intervene and end the hijacking. When it refused to do so (or, as was in fact the case, when it collaborated with the terrorists), the right to act automatically passed to Israel and to France (most of the passengers were Israeli; the airplane was French). Since France was not considering any military move (although it helped in gathering intelligence), Israel had a perfect right to take action.

This is at odds with a widely held view that national sovereignty is absolute and cannot be violated. But of course it is not absolute. Countries do not have the right to do *anything* within their borders. They risk the intervention of other states if they fail to live up to their *international* (and sometimes, in the case of intolerable human rights violations or wholesale murder, their *domestic*) obligations. Once a government agrees to receive a hijacked plane or ship, it is imposing upon itself an obligation to end the crisis without capitulation.

But what if the government has not yet developed the military competence to cope with a hostage crisis? Although this is no longer the case practically anywhere in the West, the question is worth considering. Sovereignty does not in any way preclude a government from asking another government to assist in or carry out a rescue operation, as, for example, the Somalis did when they requested the intervention of West Germany's anti-terrorist unit in the Mogadishu incident, or as other governments have done in several crises by inviting the British SAS unit to advise and assist them. In most cases of international hostage-taking, therefore, even weak or hesitant governments have a choice. Bluntly put, they either do it themselves or let someone else do it. Most of the time the real question is not one of means but of courage.

It is precisely in terrorist crises of this type that military co-operation between states could prove especially useful. By definition, ad hoc arrangements are flawed. They risk confusion, poor coordination between units of different counties, and the inevitable competition over who does what. A good way of thinking about this problem is to inquire what would happen to Western Europe in the event of a sudden Warsaw Pact onslaught— without NATO. The purpose of NATO is a common defense through two means, *coordination* of disparate forces and unified *command*. In addressing the problem of terrorism, unified command is less important. (The political reality of the West does not make that likely.) But the concept of common defense and the value of coordination are equally pertinent to the worldwide fight against international terrorism. Rather than wait, say, for the next hostage crisis, governments could prepare plans and forces to address future emergencies. They could, for example, train together, familiarize themselves with each other's bases and transport, agree on military communications methods, and exchange techniques.

Obviously, those exchanges will not be complete. The military of each country will understandably keep certain things to themselves. Even within NATO, for example, not all intelligence is shared. And yet the pooling of intelligence, and decisions based on this shared intelligence, has tremendous value. Such cooperation in gathering intelligence against terrorists is already taking place among many of the democracies, including several states outside NATO. It has prevented countless terrorist attacks and has helped foil many others. What I am proposing is to expand and formalize this cooperation.

International terrorists are emboldened when they believe that vast geographic distances protect them from any possible retaliation. But among them, the democracies of North and South America, Europe, the Middle East, and Central Asia could gird the globe. Even a cursory glance at the map tells us that America, when attempting the rescue of the hostages in Tehran in 1979, could have been assisted greatly by cooperation with Israel or, possibly, Turkey. Institutionalized cooperation could deprive terrorists and terrorist states of the assurance of military immunity which they have too often enjoyed. But it is not only shared military logistics, even of a few countries, that would act as a deterrent. It is the creation of a *common doctrine* against terrorism. The development and refinement of tactical cooperation would cement the common resolve and the common assumptions of the West in this battle. It should of course work the other way around—the Western countries should create a broad NATO-like structure, and then work out the details. But it does not. The West is unlikely to unify overnight. What is entirely feasible, however, is for the United States to begin, with two or three or possibly more countries, such an anti-terrorist alliance. Others would soon join.

How fast that happens depends on the interaction between the terrorist challenge and the Western response. Terrorism follows an inexorable, built-in escalation. To be effective, it must continually horrify and stupefy. Yet once we have become accustomed to a particular level of violence, a new outrage is required to shock our sensibilities. It used to be enough for terrorists to hijack a plane to attract international attention; next it became necessary to kill a few hostages; in the future, more violence will be required. Unchallenged, terrorism is thus likely to grow. It may achieve dimensions, in violence and in threats to the international order, which we have not yet encountered.

But equally, these new outrages are likely to induce, and may have already begun to induce, the very responses necessary to galvanize the West. For beyond a certain level of violence, the public demand for resolute action against terrorists becomes too strong to be ignored even by the most timid governments. Western governments that will lag too far behind this public sentiment will be open to sharp attack from abroad and, more important, from domestic critics and adversaries. They will come under heavy pressure to alter their policies and be more receptive to international initiatives. The escalation of terrorism thus produces the seeds of its own demise. Still, even with the likely accumulation of pressures, the actual start of an effective international campaign against terrorism is up to a *decision* of the victims, to the summoning of their collective will.

Terrorists and the states that support them are serious adversaries. They are devious, ruthless, and persistent. But I do not believe that I am in any way underestimating the threat they pose when I say that in fighting them the major problem confronting the West is its own disunity. For too long terrorists have succeeded in the strategy of divide and conquer. Governments have cut separate deals with terrorists, allowing them, for example, freedom of movement in exchange for promises of immunity. But terrorists, who by their very nature ridicule the notion of law and treaties, *always* violate their agreements. The Western countries must face up to a simple truth: *No* deals are possible with terrorism. The success of terrorism in one part of the world encourages terrorists everywhere. Terrorism is an indivisible problem, and the fight against terrorism must be indivisible as well.

This means that you cannot condone or accept, or even "understand," terrorism when directed against someone else while opposing it when directed against yourself. Terrorism threatens the foundation of lawful and humane existence everywhere. And it thrives on weakness. It is naïve to think that the IRA does not take note of periodic British courtings of the PLO. The same applies for the Red Brigades vis-à-vis the Italian government and its dealings with Arab terrorists, and so on.

What is required is a basic realignment of international attitudes toward terrorism. While all governments uniformly offer rhetorical opposition to terrorism, including the adoption of a United Nations resolution condemning terrorism in 1985, in practice they fall into one of three categories: A few governments actually *oppose* terrorism, and do so consistently; others actively *support* terrorists; but most fall into a third broad category, the *neutrals*. They either acquiesce in terrorism or refuse outright to oppose it. A proper policy toward terrorism must take into account each of these types of states.

I have already discussed measures that can be taken against states that support terrorism. But equally fundamental is the need to do away with the middle ground of neutrality. We must force a dichotomy. Governments must be made to understand that if they acquiesce in terrorism they are in practice supporting it. For example, the provision of safe passage to foreign terrorists (such as offered by Egypt to the hijackers of the *Achille Lauro*) should be considered an act of simple collusion. It is tantamount to offering a foreign army passage through your territory in time of war. The claim of neutrality, a problematic moral posture in wartime anyway, breaks down completely in this case. Similarly, accepting a hijacked airplane or ship without accepting the concomitant responsibility of preventing the

escape of the terrorists is also an act of collusion; as is the refusal
to extradite or punish terrorists, or, in many instances, to rescue
hostages.

The provision of sanctuary for terrorists is also an act of collusion. I am not talking about taking in refugees (such as France
did after the Spanish Civil War). I am talking about letting armed
bands wage terrorist war from one's borders against a neigh-
boring state. This is *not* one of the privileges of sovereignty. It
is a clear act of aggression. It can and should be treated as such
by the attacked state, which has every right to take action against
the terrorists or the government that shelters them. It may do
so either in hot pursuit, in retaliation, or when faced with a
mounting threat, in preemptive action. Just as terrorists must
be deprived of the civilian shield afforded by the absolute inhibition against civilian casualties, they must be deprived of the
political sanctuary afforded by an absolutist definition of sovereignty. The right of self-defense takes precedence over the
claim of territorial sovereignty.

Thus, Morocco's action against the terrorists launched from
Algeria is justified. As was Oman's action (assisted by the British)
against terrorists launched from South Yemen in the 1970s. Nor
is this type of action limited to contiguous borders. Israel's strike
against the PLO headquarters in Tunisia in 1985 was based on
exactly the same principle.

When a state deliberately employs terrorists, the distinction
between striking back at the terrorists themselves or at the governments that shelter them is one of practical consideration, not
of principle. There is certainly no moral imperative to *confine*
the retaliation to the actual perpetrators; the terrorists, after all,
are merely servants of the government. In war, limiting a coun-
terattack to exactly those soldiers who fired at you would be the
height of folly. For one thing, military units change their positions frequently, especially after they launch an attack (such as
a bombardment or an armed foray) to avoid a counterstrike. No
military commander in his right mind would accept the notion
that unless he can locate the exact artillery battery, the exact
commando base from which an attack was launched, he may not

respond. The aggressor would thus continually escape retaliation.

Yet this is precisely the notion that the governments sponsoring terrorism are trying to foist, not without success, on the West. (Part of that success may be attributed to a willingness by some to seize this argument as a pretext for avoiding action.) If a government has harbored, trained, and launched terrorists, it becomes the legitimate object of a military response.

The public discussion on this matter typically falls into a legalistic pitfall. We are told we cannot prove conclusively such involvement with terrorists. This very often is simply not true. Western governments already possess ample intelligence evidence (such as satellite photos of training camps, interception of communications, reports from agents in the field) of continuous support for terrorists from certain governments. Such a record of complicity is more than strong enough to morally justify punitive action against these criminal states. There are plenty of military or strategic targets that can be struck to inflict sharp damage, while avoiding excessive, if any, civilian casualties.

Two objections are frequently raised. First, the prospect of reprisals. Qaddafi, for example, who harbored Abu Nidal prior to his attacks on Americans and others in European airports in 1985, promised to retaliate if the United States took any action against him. (He went so far as to promise to set the Mediterranean ablaze and even to precipitate global war.) Such bluster should be viewed realistically. It is more than mere grandstanding; it emanates from fear. It also at times may be partly realized. We should recognize a sober truth: A successful war on terrorism will involve a succession of blows and counterblows, and some unavoidable casualties along the way. What is required is a commitment to a *continuous* campaign against its sponsors, not just erratic responses to individual terrorist acts. There are no one-shot solutions. A forceful response against aggression may very well elicit reprisals initially. But over the long run, it is the only way to make governments stop launching terrorist killers. They need to know, they *must* know, that the West will not sit back and take it.

The second objection raised against military action against states sponsoring terrorism is that it will induce political consequences unfavorable to the West, such as, in the Middle East, the weakening or collapse of friendly regimes. The point is often lost that these very regimes, notwithstanding their public pronouncements, would secretly welcome such action; after all, they too are frequent victims of the terrorist war. Still, what about unfavorable political developments? In many regions of the world, especially the Middle East, anger precedes respect. There may be a lashing out at Western or pro-Western targets following a military action, but there is a concomitant, if grudging, assessment of new limits. A posture of weakness, a repeated refusal to confront and punish the regimes behind the terrorists, not only invites further aggression but ultimately *weakens* the West's position, and consequently the position of its allies, in these regions and throughout the world.

But what if a state is *coerced* by terrorists to offer its territory for attacks? That is, in fact, what happened to Lebanon when the PLO effectively turned it into a terrorist base against Israel. The answer is quite clear. Sovereignty imposes not only the right but the obligation to control one's territory. This is, in fact, what Hussein had to do in Jordan in September 1970, when he was in danger of losing control of the country to the PLO. If he had not defeated the PLO, Israel would have had to do so. In contrast, when Lebanon could not discharge its obligation in 1982, Israel had every right to forcibly intervene to remove the PLO bases in Lebanon.

Going after individual terrorists in countries that refuse to arrest or extradite them is merely a specific application of this principle. The American interception of the Egyptian plane carrying the PLO terrorists who held Americans hostage and killed one of them was thus both necessary and just. The claim that this was a violation of Egypt's sovereignty and civil aviation rights is nonsense. Such rights are not accorded to shield killers on the run. Embassies, airplanes, ships, and sovereign territory are not endowed with any special dispensation to be used for such purposes. And when they are abused, they automatically forfeit any immunities they would normally have. Terrorists and their backers would have us believe that sovereignty and diplomatic immunity are the modern equivalents of the horns of the altar in the Bible. By grasping at them, they think they will be given immunity after the most terrible crimes. Like Solomon, we should simply refuse to obey.

But even lesser forms of tolerating terrorism, such as a laxity or a refusal to maintain proper security safeguards in airports, should be considered a tacit form of collusion with terrorists. It allows them to penetrate the air routes and attack civilians from all countries. Governments that do not uphold their security obligations should be told that their airports will be cut off from the rest of the international aviation system until they improve security.

The broad assortment of states who engage in all, or even some, of these "neutral" acts must be told that they, too, will be held up to a higher standard. If they repeatedly, or as a matter of policy, facilitate the operations of terrorists, they risk being subjected to some or all of the sanctions that outright supporters of terrorists invite upon themselves.

Such a policy of firmness will make it clear that individual terrorists will be pursued, caught, and punished; that the organizations that launch them will be subject to attack; that the governments that shelter them will face political, economic, and, if necessary, military retaliation; that other governments that collude less brazenly will also be held accountable.

What, then, has inhibited the widespread adoption of this policy by the West? I believe it is the persistent effects of two vices. One is greed, or a heedless promotion of economic self-interest, whatever the political or moral consequences. The other is political cowardice, which means sitting it out while your ally is attacked, or responds to an attack, so as not to invoke the wrath of the terrorists. Both tendencies influenced the unfavorable response to the American initiative for sanctions against Libya in 1986 following the attacks on the Rome and Vienna airports. Neither cowardice nor greed will easily disappear. If, however, the United States persists in its firm stance, over time a common policy for the West would eventually emerge, pressuring, even shaming, Western states into compliance.

But there is a third, even more pernicious impediment that needs to be overcome: a confusion that is both moral and intellectual. It stems from our nature as citizens of political societies. We believe in the capacity of politics to mitigate, and resolve, all conflict. We automatically tend to endow an adversary with the same assumptions. These could not be more misplaced than in the case of terrorists, who use political language to destroy the concept of politics altogether. And even when we catch a glimpse of this truth, we fail to grasp its essence. For the West is in awe of fanaticism. It is confused before a putative willingness to die for a cause, believing that such readiness must be based on a cause that is at least partially just. Even a cursory reading of history tells us how dangerous a notion that is.

But how do we form our opinions of the present? The West depends in large measure on its media. This is why terrorists, in their war against the West, devote so much of their strategy and their effort to capturing the Western press and using it for their own purposes. But this need not be a one-way street. Terrorism's unique reliance on the press and television of the democracies gives them tremendous power to amplify terrorism's message *or to snuff it out*. It has been said, correctly, that the Western media have a penchant to legitimize terrorists by treating them as respectable political adversaries and their claims as worthy of serious consideration. But the media's capacity to do such damage is the mirror image of their capacity to do good. They can and should refuse to broadcast interviews with terrorists uncritically. They can and should expose the sham of terrorist claims. They can and should expose their grisly acts for what they are. Should? Some say we cannot use that word in relation to a free press. I fail to see why citizens cannot scrutinize and criticize journalists. Scrutiny is not censorship. What the public has a right to demand of journalists is the same scrupulousness and professionalism, no more and no less, that they would show in the case of covering organized crime and its bosses. The proven power of a thorough press investigation to expose and repudiate such corruption—indeed, to galvanize public opposition against it—is exactly the power that can be harnessed against terrorism. A thoughtful press can turn terrorism's greatest weapon against the terrorists themselves.

This is the responsibility of the West's press. It is second only to the responsibility of its political leadership. For only a determined leadership can make the West overcome its three impediments—greed, cowardice, and moral confusion. Which leadership? It can only come from the United States, which alone has the capacity to align the West in this matter, alone can credibly threaten the offenders, and alone can impel the neutrals to shed their neutrality. The United States appears to be moving precisely in this direction, albeit sometimes at a maddeningly slow pace. America encountered terrorism in the middle 1960s. By the middle 1970s, it realized it was its principal target. By the middle 1980s, it began thinking seriously about taking action. The more America resorts to action, such as punishing terrorists and their backers, the greater the number of states which will join the effort to combat terrorism. Allies and adversaries alike, the entire world in fact, are waiting to see the depth of American resolve.

The West can win the war against terrorism, and fairly rapidly. It can expose its duplicity and punish its perpetrators and sponsors. But it must first win the war against its own inner weakness. That will require courage. We shall need at least three types of it.

First, statesmen and government leaders must have the political courage to present the truth, however unpleasant, to their people. They must be prepared to make difficult decisions, to take measures that may involve great risks, that may even end in failure and subject them to public criticism.

Second, the soldiers who may actually be called upon to combat terrorists will need to show military courage. They are usually members of special units created precisely for such tasks. It will be up to them to decide whether they can or cannot undertake a particular operation a government is considering. In the special units of the Israeli army, for example, no one has ever been simply *told* by the political leadership that he would have to accept a perilous assignment. The commanders of the unit were always *asked*: Is it possible? Do you think you can do it? And if they had said it could not be done, or even if they had expressed doubts, that would have been the end of the matter. The political leaders would have called the mission off. This was the case in Entebbe and in countless other actions that dealt stunning defeats to international terrorism.

But there is also a third kind of courage: the civic valor that must be shown by an entire people. All citizens in a democracy threatened by terrorism must see themselves, in a certain sense, as soldiers in a common battle. They must not pressure their government to capitulate or to surrender to terrorism. This is especially true of public pressure on government by families of hostages. Such pressure can only be called a dereliction of civic duty. If we seriously want to win the war against terrorism, people must be prepared to endure sacrifice and even, should there be the loss of loved ones, immeasurable pain.

Terrorism is a phenomenon which tries to evoke one feeling: fear. It is understandable that the one virtue most necessary to defeat terrorism is therefore the antithesis of fear: courage.

Courage, said the Romans, is not the only virtue, but it is the single virtue without which all the others are meaningless.

The terrorist challenge must be answered. The choice is between a free society based on law and compassion and a rampant barbarism in the service of brute force and tyranny. Confusion and vacillation facilitated the rise of terrorism. Clarity and courage will ensure its defeat.

APPENDIX

APPENDIX

Terrorism and the Media

A Symposium

From the Jonathan Institute's Conference on International
Terrorism, Washington, D.C.
June 26, 1984

TED KOPPEL: Let me begin by putting forward the proposition
that the media, particularly television, and terrorists need one
another, that they have what is fundamentally a symbiotic relationship. Without television, international terrorism becomes
rather like the philosopher's hypothetical tree falling in the
forest—no one hears it fall and therefore it doesn't exist. And
television without terrorism, while not deprived of all the interesting things in the world, is nonetheless deprived of one of
the most interesting.

NORMAN PODHORETZ: Certainly terrorists and the media have
had such a relationship, which has helped give the lie to those
pious proclamations on the editorial pages that organizations like
the PLO, by engaging in terrorism, hurt their own cause. On
the contrary, it is clear that, for a long time, because of this
symbiotic relationship, the power and influence of such organizations increased with each new terrorist act.

In the last few years, however, this relationship has been
disrupted by what I call Robert Nisbet's law, which states that
boredom is the most underrated force in human affairs. After
the ten thousandth hijacking or wanton assassination, the media
have become bored, and their coverage has accordingly declined. Much less attention is paid to terrorist episodes these

[229]

days than even five years ago. Insofar as this prevents terrorist
organizations from achieving their principal objective, which is
to get a lot of publicity, this development is good news. But it
also indicates how accustomed the public has grown to these
acts: we are no longer as horrified by them as we should be.
Terrorist outrages are now taken for granted, as are the subtle
exculpations that the media help propagate, for example, that
terrorism represents a protest against intolerable social conditions or that it is a form of guerrilla warfare. Such exculpations
have so taken hold that they now govern the public's response
to terrorism.

CHARLES KRAUTHAMMER: I think Norman Podhoretz is right in
saying that a kind of boredom is setting in. "Normal" airplane
hijackings, for example, are now covered on the inside pages of
most newspapers. But terrorists are rather resourceful about
creating new theatrical productions; every year or two they come
up with a new variant that captures the media's imagination.
The most recent innovation is the suicide bombing, such as the
attack on the American Marines in Lebanon and on the U.S.
embassy in Kuwait.

But we should remember that not all terrorism is dependent
on the media. When we discuss terrorism we are really talking
about at least three different kinds of political violence. The first
and oldest kind is assassination, the usual form of political violence before World War II. The political assassin often does not
need the media to explain what his act means; in fact, his principal objective may not be publicity at all. His goal is simply to
eliminate a political actor.

The second form of terrorism, which emerged after the war,
is the random attack on civilians, but civilians of a particular
type—civilians who are members of the enemy class or nationality. Terrorism of this sort, as practiced, for example, by the
FLN in Algeria in the 1950s and the early 1960s, is also independent of the media. Its object is to demoralize the enemy
during a war, and its audience is the victims themselves and
their compatriots.

The third and newest form of terrorism, which the PLO largely created after 1968, is the random attack on anyone. We might refer to this as "media terrorism," for it can exist only if there is an interpreter to give it meaning. The terrorist acts of the PLO were at bottom not intended to demoralize the Israelis but to publicize political grievances. The intended audience was not the immediate victims—the airline passengers, or even the Israelis—but the entire world. For such actions, coverage by the mass media becomes absolutely essential. This is where the terrorists' utter dependence on the media begins.

The media's responsibility to act with self-restraint is obviously greatest with this kind of terrorism. In those cases where the victim is chosen at random and has no connection whatever with any political struggle, terrorism is actually a lure to attract the media. Through his acts, the terrorist tries to earn a stage on which to proclaim his message. And the media then undertake the task of interpreting those acts. In 1979, for example, terrorists attacked the American embassy in Beirut with grenades. One network correspondent explained that this action was "perhaps an expression of resentment and frustration" on the part of Palestinians over the Israeli–Egyptian peace treaty. Here we reach a level where an attack on innocents is rationalized as a psychological necessity.

Consider the coastal road massacre in Israel. It was generally explained as the PLO's assertion that it still existed after its expulsion from Lebanon—a kind of "I kill, therefore I am." Without the press to carry this message, the act would have been meaningless; in fact, since it had no military or political purpose, it probably would not have been committed in the first place. When the point of a terrorist attack is to force the media to function as interpreters, the media have a heavy responsibility not to do the interpreting.

KOPPEL: Mr. O'Sullivan, would you comment on the conflict that arises when a democracy confronts terrorism. Does one oppose terrorism by using methods that are non-democratic, such as censoring the press, or by so doing does one undermine democracy itself?

JOHN O'SULLIVAN: A directive, issued by Conor Cruise O'Brien when he was Minister of Posts and Telegraphs, forbids the broadcasting of interviews with IRA members. Why? Because, as Dr. O'Brien has said, "We in the Irish state regard the appearance of terrorists on television as an incitement to murder. The incitement is addressed not so much to the general public as to other terrorists and potential terrorists." Such appearances glamorize these people. Since they have little support among the population, they would not be invited to give their views on television and be treated respectfully if they had not engaged in a campaign of murder.

I would be perfectly prepared to support a ban on interviews with terrorists in Northern Ireland, since the only justification advanced for such interviews—namely, that we need to know what the terrorists' views are—is absurd. We know what their views are before they ever appear on television.

KOPPEL: Daniel Schorr, can such limits on the media be legitimately imposed in a democracy?

DANIEL SCHORR: What Charles Krauthammer said is true: there was terrorism before there was television. Lincoln was assassinated in the Ford Theater, Archduke Ferdinand was assassinated in Sarajevo, and television wasn't there, although I am sure it would like to have been. But in our society television and violence have a mutual attraction that is very, very dangerous. Television has become the arbiter of who is important, who has identity. Many people have found that the royal road to identity is to do something violent. Television has a love affair with drama.

Being on television confers a kind of notoriety on people, much more so than being written about in the newspaper. But what should TV journalists do? Not cover terrorist events? Obviously not—we are in the news business. But we don't have to provide live coverage when nothing is really happening. We don't have to telephone terrorists and ask them to give live interviews. We in the news business should impose some voluntary limits, because if we don't there may come a time when they are imposed on us.

GEORGE WILL: To think that the press holds the key to the problems of terrorism is not uncustomary narcissism on the part of the journalistic profession. What can we really do to diminish the incentive for publicity? I suggest precious little. If terrorists take over an embassy in the center of London, or seize an American ambassador, or shoot a Pope, people are going to notice. It doesn't matter whether you have a policy about how many hours you're on the air. Terrorists will achieve their magnifying effect, which is what they use the media for. And in a country that is blessed—or, depending on your point of view, afflicted—with a First Amendment, it is quite impossible, given how the law has recently been construed, to enforce any kind of prior restraint. Absent enforcement from a fourth party, the competition between competitive media virtually guarantees that there will be maximum coverage of anything spectacular and telegenic.

Perhaps one problem lies in our definition of the term "terrorist." I don't think we ought to say that John Wilkes Booth or Gavrilo Princip were terrorists, although certainly they had political aims. The dominant kind of terrorism today, the kind we should be discussing, is what Secretary of State Shultz has called state-sponsored terrorism. Such terrorism is used by certain states as an instrument of national policy. It is only the beginning of clarity to understand that just as revolutions are made not by bad water or bad schools or hungry people but by revolutionaries, so terrorism is made not by television but by terrorists. Terrorists make terrorism for the same reason people make potato chips—it pays. When it doesn't pay, they'll quit making terrorism. And I think it would be a mistake to assume that the public is apt to grow bored very soon. The "Indiana Jones phenomenon" will undoubtedly come to affect terrorism—that is, just when the senses of the public seem saturated, terrorists will find new ways to lacerate people's sensibilities.

BOB WOODWARD: First, I don't think we are talking only about television, as Daniel Schorr said. We have to ask ourselves what sort of terrorism is politically most significant. I agree with George Will that it is the state-supported variety, and I think television is largely irrelevant to that. Consider the assassination of

President-elect Bashir Gemayel in Lebanon in 1982. American intelligence agencies have established that the assassination was carried out by Syrian intelligence officers, and a credible case can be made that President Assad of Syria ordered it. Now this was a very alarming event. It changed the history and the politics of Lebanon. You don't need television to convey its importance, or that of the bombing of the Marines in Beirut. The importance of the bombing was its military effect, not the fact that it was spectacular TV. I think the journalist's role in covering such events, whether he is a television reporter or a newspaper reporter, remains the traditional one—finding out who is responsible for them and then broadcasting or printing that information.

ALAIN BESANÇON: Perhaps our real problem here is not so much defining terrorism as understanding the effect that terrorism publicized by the media can have on society. After all, most terrorism is undertaken in order to arouse the sympathy of society. So the question involves not simply journalism but the basic philosophical assumptions that are shared by the leaders of the cultural establishment. The ideology of most terrorist groups holds that Western capitalist society is doomed and does not deserve to be defended, or that from its destruction something more worthwhile will emerge. This was the philosophy of the first large-scale terrorist movement, that of the Russian populists in the 1800s. Even Tolstoy, who espoused non-violence, admired the ideas behind this movement. Or consider Jean-Paul Sartre, who applauded the terrorism of the Baader-Meinhof gang in Germany and the Red Brigades in Italy. He believed that there was a continuity between the eschatological hope of the terrorist and the reasonable need we all recognize to correct the flaws that exist in our society. I think this kind of sublime morality is very widespread and very difficult to eradicate. It is beyond the ability of the media to do so. This belief is most common among the highly educated, and it is from this group that most journalists and the leaders of the so-called cultural establishment are drawn.

O'SULLIVAN: This panel is composed of journalists from what is called the quality press. But I suggest that the reporting on terrorism in the so-called popular press is often more accurate than it is in the more serious newspapers. Let's consider how each would describe an IRA bombing attack.

Popular newspapers like the New York *Post* or the *Daily Mail* in England might say: "A shy 21-year-old girl, whose only interest in life is tennis, was last night fighting for her life in a London hospital after being blown up in a restaurant by an IRA bomb. By her bedside was her fiancé, Gordon Williamson, 23. 'She didn't have an enemy in the world,' he said."

The New York Times or the *Guardian* would report something quite different: "Two people were killed and one injured in an IRA explosion in London last night. Government sources interpreted the explosion as a response to the government's decision to introduce a bill increasing parliamentary representation for Ulster. Sources in Belfast believed to be close to the IRA said that the attack was the start of a major campaign in which targets on the British mainland would not be exempt."

The assumption of the popular press is that terrorists are important for what they *do*. The assumption of the quality press is that terrorists are important for what they *say*. I suggest that the first assumption is much more sensible—that terrorists are criminals rather than politicians.

LORD CHALFONT: Perhaps the real problem with the media, or at least with the quality press, is its tendency to adopt a position of magisterial objectivity between our society and those attacking it. Norman Podhoretz said that the media subtly excuse certain terrorist acts by implying that they arise out of intolerable social conditions or intolerable oppression. We see these justifications as well in the media's tendency to equate the actions of legitimate governments, such as that in El Salvador, in fighting terrorists and revolutionaries with the activities of the revolutionaries themselves. Can we not simply accept the fact that there are two sides, ours and theirs? If their side prevails, our freedoms will disappear, and the first freedom to go will be freedom of the press. Is it too much to ask that, in a free society at war with international terrorism, the press should be on our side?

KRAUTHAMMER: Yes, it is too much to ask. Unless the press takes the position that terrorism, defined as the indiscriminate attack on innocents to achieve political ends, is absolutely indefensible, a moral corruption begins that is irreversible. If we compromise that principle, then our assertion that we stand for certain values is a hollow one, because high among those values is the belief that civilians ought to be exempt from attack. If there are people on our side who engage in the murder of civilians—for example, the gangsters who practice terrorism in El Salvador—they have to be condemned with as much vigor as those who do it in the name of another ideology.

The rule of thumb I propose is this: In covering terrorist events, reporters ought to concentrate on who, what, where, and when. They should leave the question of why to the historians and the psychiatrists.

WOODWARD: I don't think any journalist would want to eliminate the "whys" from any story.

SCHORR: We've been talking as if the problem is undue interference by the media, whereas the problem is really how terrorists manipulate the media. People who feel that the newspapers they read and the television news they watch should reflect their own personal views are making a grave mistake. If we adopt this line of thinking, we will eventually have the kind of press that exists in Paris—a partisan press in which everyone can find his own views reflected in his newspaper.

What is the responsibility of the press in covering terrorism? If a representative of a terrorist group approaches *The Washington Post* and says, "I want to try to explain to you who we are and what we are," Bob Woodward can write a gripping story describing who the terrorists are and what they believe. By writing this story he does not prevent the police from taking action against them. But if the government then forces him to betray the confidence that made the story possible, so that a few people may be arrested, he will never get that kind of story again. Some of us still believe that journalists are people committed to the idea that the world must *know*. We believe that our job is to explain who terrorists are without accepting the

view of any one side. The free press can be destroyed very easily
if it is polarized in the way some have suggested here. We should
examine the press in countries where it tries to satisfy the prej-
udices of particular groups—in France, the Soviet Union, Syria—
before we start making new rules for ourselves.

WILL: I believe, as Charles Krauthammer has said elsewhere,
that we should apply a sort of Heisenberg principle to the media.
We in the media do effectively observe, but what we tend to
observe, more often than events themselves, is the observers.
We have heard today that the press has a double standard in
covering terrorism. I think the alarming news is that there is a
single standard. You cannot underestimate the degree to which
both sides, liberal and conservative, have a common view of the
world that they simply cannot bear to have the fact of international terrorism challenged. The view involves denial of the
undeniable—the fact that we are under assault from the Soviet
Union. That is how I read Claire Sterling's book on international
terrorism, *The Terror Network*. Very few people, of whatever
political persuasion, are willing to accept the reality of international terrorism. Our whole political culture has an enormous
intellectual, psychological, and emotional investment in a view
of the world that the fact of international terrorism challenges.
The media did not create this view; they merely serve to reflect
the larger culture in which it is embedded.

PODHORETZ: It has been said that the media should change the
rules. I submit that the rules have already been changed. Some
years back, the attitudes of the popular press that John O'Sullivan
described were prevalent in the quality press as well. There was
a time when our political culture was, in fact, a partisan of our
side, when the journalist's role as a citizen did not conflict with
his professional role. But in the later years of the Vietnam War
this began to change. The passionate speeches we hear about
objectivity and freedom of the press ring rather hollow today,
because there is very little objectivity in the reporting of terrorist
acts. Very often the terms that are used to characterize terrorists
reveal a mindless bias—when Yasir Arafat is referred to as a
moderate, for example. The media have become the most prom-

inent exponents of these attitudes in the larger political culture, and I think this accounts for the widespread resentment of the press and TV. Many, many people, including myself, feel that the media are unsympathetic to our side in the struggle against totalitarianism in general and totalitarian communism in particular.

KRAUTHAMMER: I find George Will uncharacteristically modest as to the importance and influence of the media. There can be no question that the development of enormously powerful communications technology in the hands of people who believe in competing with one another to get a good story has produced a new phenomenon. The American hostages would not have been held so long had the Iranians not realized that they had created the most effective television stage in history, which gave them immediate access to millions of people. The Iranians exploited the hostage crisis in a way that they could not have done in the absence of television cameras.

I want to give an example of the sort of media self-restraint that I am suggesting. In the late 1970s, there was a rash of episodes in which spectators at sporting events jumped out onto the playing field for their fifteen seconds of exposure on national television. After a number of these episodes, some of the networks decided to turn the cameras away. Instead, a reporter would say, "There's someone running onto the field, but we won't show him to you because if we do, it will encourage other clowns to do the same thing." Now, when you hear the crowd cheering as the clowns are being chased off the field, you really want to see what is happening. But clearly it is worth forgoing that pleasure in order to gain a greater societal good—the non-disruption of future ball games. I think the media executives should exercise the same self-restraint in covering media terrorism, when the societal good to be gained is reducing the incentive to political murder.

KOPPEL: There is a great need to be aware of the proper roles in our society of journalists as well as of political leaders. When our leaders don't play the roles they should be playing, then the media are put in a totally irrational position. After all, it is not

the job of the media to censor themselves. Vietnam was mentioned a few minutes ago. Press censorship was never imposed
during the Vietnam War because President Johnson was unwilling to pay the political price of a declaration of war. If indeed
our leaders believe that we are in a state of war, then let it be
declared. Once war is declared, then all kinds of societal pressures, and indeed legal pressures, come to bear on the media
to play a different role from the one they play right now.

But I urge you not to be in too much of a hurry to change the
role that we in the media play, because once it has been changed,
even for reasons that now seem valid, it may be difficult to change
it back when the reasons are no longer so valid.

Contributors

Moshe Arens is a minister in the Israeli government, and served as Minister of Defense. He was Israel's Ambassador to the United States and chairman of the Knesset's Defense and Foreign Relations Committee.

Jillian Becker has written a number of books about terrorism, including *PLO: Rise and Fall of the Palestine Liberation Organization* and *The Soviet Union and Terrorism.*

Walter Berns has taught constitutional law at Yale, Cornell, the University of Toronto, the University of Chicago, and Georgetown University. His books include *The First Amendment, The Future of American Democracy,* and *For Capital Punishment.*

Alain Besançon is Professor of the History of Russian Culture at the Ecole des Hautes Etudes in Paris. His books include *The Intellectual Origins of Lenin* and *The Soviet Syndrome.*

Yehuda Z. Blum is Professor of International Law and has taught at the Hebrew University, where he held the Lauterpacht Chair; at New York University; and at the University of Texas. He served as Israel's Ambassador to the United Nations from 1978 to 1984. His books include *Historic Titles in International Law* and *Secure Boundaries and Middle East Peace.*

Arnaud de Borchgrave is editor in chief of the *Washington Times* and was chief foreign correspondent of *Newsweek.* His books include *The Spike* and *Monimbo.*

Lord Chalfont is a former Cabinet Minister in the British government. He is the author of several works, including a biography of Field Marshal Montgomery and an analysis of American military power, *The Sword and the Spirit*.

Alan Cranston is U.S. Senator from California and Democratic Whip. He has served on major committees in the U.S. Senate, including the Foreign Relations Committee and the Arms Control Subcommittee.

Midge Decter is executive director of the Committee for the Free World. Her works include *The Liberated Woman and Other Americans*, *The New Chastity*, and *Liberal Parents, Radical Children*.

Wolfgang Fikentscher is Professor of Law at the University of Munich. He has taught at the universities of Munster, Tübingen, Michigan, and California. He has written numerous works on legality, anarchy, and international relations.

Arthur J. Goldberg is a former Associate Justice of the U.S. Supreme Court, former U.S. Permanent Representative to the United Nations, and former Secretary of Labor. He currently practices international law.

Paul Johnson is a British writer and historian. He was editor of *The New Statesman*. His books include *A History of Christianity* and *Modern Times*.

Elie Kedourie is Professor of Politics at the University of London and teaches at the London School of Economics. He is the editor of the quarterly *Middle Eastern Studies*. His books include *Nationalism in Asia and Africa*, *Islam in the Modern World and Other Studies*, and *The Chatham House Version and Other Studies*.

Jack Kemp is a Congressman from New York. He has served as chairman of the House Republican Committee and as the ranking Republican on the Foreign Operations Committee. He was a congressional delegate to the SALT talks and to the U.S. Commission on Refugees.

Jeane J. Kirkpatrick was U.S. Ambassador to the United Nations. She has been Professor of Government at Georgetown University. Her books include *Dictatorship and Double Standards: Rationalism and Reason in Politics* and *The New Presidential Elite*.

Leszek Kolakowski was for many years Professor of the History of Philosophy at the University of Warsaw. Since his expulsion from Poland, he has divided his time between All Souls College, Oxford, and the University of Chicago. His books include *Main Currents of Marxism* and *Religion*.

Ted Koppel is anchorman for ABC News *Nightline* and *Viewpoint*. He was ABC's chief diplomatic correspondent, anchorman for the *ABC Saturday Night News*, and Bureau Chief in Tokyo and Hong Kong.

Charles Krauthammer is senior editor at *The New Republic* magazine, a contributing essayist to *Time*, and a columnist for *The Washington Post*. He is the author of *Cutting Edges*.

Paul Laxalt has been senior United States Senator from Nevada and chairman of the Republican Party. He has served on the Appropriations and Judiciary Committees and as chairman of the Judiciary Criminal Law Subcommittee.

Michael Ledeen is a senior fellow at the Georgetown Center for Strategic and International Studies and the former executive editor of *The Washington Quarterly*. He has taught at Washington University and at the University of Rome. His books include *Debacle: The American Failure in Iran* and *Grave New World*.

Burton Leiser is Professor of Philosophy and Professor of Law at Pace University. His books include *Custom, Law, and Morality* and *Values in Conflict: Life, Liberty, and the Rule of Law*.

Bernard Lewis is Cleveland E. Dodge Professor of Near Eastern Studies, Princeton University, and a member of the Institute for Advanced Study at Princeton. His books include *The Origins of Ismailism, The Arabs in History, The Middle East and the West, The Assassins*, and *The Muslim Discovery of Europe*. He is co-editor of *The Cambridge History of Islam* and *The Encyclopedia of Islam*.

Christian Lochte is director of the Hamburg Senate and the chief of the Office for the Protection of the Constitution, West Germany's agency responsible for combating terrorism.

Edwin Meese III is Attorney General of the United States and was Counsellor to the President. He was formerly Professor of Law at the University of San Diego, where he was also director of the Center for Criminal Justice Policy and Management.

Daniel Patrick Moynihan is senior United States Senator from New York. He has served as Vice Chairman of the Senate Select Committee on Intelligence. He was U.S. Ambassador to the United Nations and to India and was Professor of Government at Harvard University. He is the author of many books, including *Beyond the Melting Pot* and *A Dangerous Place*.

Takeshi Muramatsu is Dean of the College of Comparative Culture at Tsukaba University. His books include *Charles de Gaulle, International Terrorism,* and *Blood, Sand, and Prayer—A History of the Contemporary Middle East.*

Benjamin Netanyahu is Israel's Ambassador to the United Nations and was deputy ambassador in Washington. He served for five years in the special forces of the Israeli army. He is the editor of *International Terrorism: Challenge and Response* and co-editor of *The Letters of Jonathan Netanyahu.*

Benzion Netanyahu is Professor Emeritus of Judaic Studies at Cornell University. He was the founding editor of the *World History of the Jewish People* and editor in chief of the *Encyclopedia Hebraica.* His works include *The Marranos of Spain* and *Don Isaac Abravanel: Statesman and Philosopher.* He was founding chairman of the Jonathan Institute.

John O'Sullivan is deputy editor of the *Times* of London. He was the editorial page editor of the New York *Post* and editor of *Policy Review.* He was formerly on the editorial staff of the London *Daily Telegraph.*

Norman Podhoretz is the editor of *Commentary* magazine. His books include *Why We Were in Vietnam, The Present Danger, Breaking Ranks: A Political Memoir,* and *The Bloody Crossroads: Where Literature and Politics Meet.*

Yitzhak Rabin is Israel's Minister of Defense. Prior to holding that post he served as Prime Minister, Ambassador to the United States, and Chief of Staff during the Six-Day War.

Jean-François Revel is the author of *How Democracies Perish, The Totalitarian Temptation, Without Marx or Jesus,* and many other books. He has taught in Mexico City, Florence, Lille, and Paris, and was editor of *L'Express.*

Eugene Rostow is Stirling Professor of Law and Dean of the Yale Law School. Among his posts in the U.S. government have been director of the Arms Control and Disarmament Agency and Under Secretary of State for Political Affairs.

Daniel Schorr was a senior correspondent for CBS and CNN and the first CBS bureau chief in Moscow. He is the author of several books, including *Clearing the Air.*

Meir Shamgar is the Chief Justice of Israel. He served as Israel's Attorney General, as Legal Advisor to the Ministry of Defense, and as Military Advocate General. He is a director of the Jonathan Institute.

George P. Shultz, the sixtieth U.S. Secretary of State, was Secretary of Labor, Director of the Office of Management and Budget, Secretary of the Treasury, and chairman of the Council on Economic Policy. He taught at M.I.T. and the University of Chicago and has published books on economics, business, and labor-management issues.

Claire Sterling is an American foreign correspondent, based in Italy for over thirty years. She has written for many of the principal international newspapers and magazines. Her books include *The Masaryk Case*, *The Terror Network*, and *The Time of the Assassins*.

P. J. Vatikiotis is Professor of Politics with Reference to the Near and Middle East at the University of London. His books include *Egypt from Muhammad Ali to Sadat*, *Arab and Regional Politics in the Middle East*, and *Nasser and His Generation*.

William H. Webster is the director of the Federal Bureau of Investigation. He has served in several judicial posts, including U.S. Attorney for the Eastern District of Missouri, and judge of the U.S. District Court and of the United States Court of Appeals.

George Will is a Pulitzer Prize-winning columnist whose articles appear in *Newsweek*, *The Washington Post*, and more than three hundred other newspapers in the United States. His books include *The Pursuit of Happiness and Other Sobering Thoughts* and *Statecraft as Soulcraft*.

Bob Woodward is assistant managing editor of *The Washington Post*. He is co-author of *All the President's Men*, *The Final Days*, *The Brethren*, and *Wired*. His six-part series, *The Terror Factor*, appeared in *The Washington Post*.

Index